Above: Just a month after the inauguration of through electric services from England to Scotland, Class 87 Bo-Bo No 87029 hurries a Birmingham-Glasgow train past Greenholme on June 8 1974. *J. H. Cooper-Smith*

Right: Passenger services on the 1500V dc Manchester-Sheffield line via Woodhead have been withdrawn but freight traffic is still very heavy. Some of the Class 76 Bo-Bos have been fitted for multiple working, and two are seen here in tandem at Hazlehead with a Merry-go-round train for Fiddler's Ferry on June 28 1970.
P. N. Bradley

Top left: Running 35 minutes late, the down morning Manchester Pullman picks its way carefully through Crewe on February 6 1974 in the charge of Class 86/2 Bo-Bo No 86230. *Philip Hawkins*

Far left: Underneath the arches of Clapton comes Class 305/1 unit No 417 at the head of a Liverpool Street-Chingford working on January 25 1972.
J. H. Cooper-Smith

Left: Sunrise over Hampton-in-Arden on January 25, 1974 finds Class 310 unit No 074 hurrying towards the Midlands metropolis on the 08·32 Coventry-Birmingham New Street working. *Philip Hawkins*

Last of the true narrow gauge?

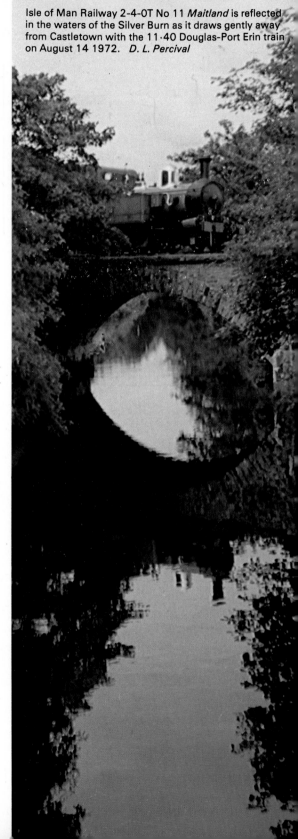

For me, true narrow gauge railway operation in this country ceased in November 1965. For in that month the Isle of Man Railway announced the "temporary" withdrawal of services for urgent maintenance, and normal services were never resumed.

I should hasten to say that I have no wish to decry the valiant efforts of the narrow gauge railway preservationists — indeed I am one of them myself — but I fear the provision of viable year-round services on narrow gauge metals in the British Isles is now an impossible task.

But what made the old IMR so different from its Welsh counterparts? I can do no better than describe my first three visits to the Island, and in fact my first taste of the 3ft gauge.

I hate crowds and, having heard tales of how busy the IMR could be at the height of the holiday season, I chose the last but one week of the winter service for my visit. One train a day ran from the capital, Douglas, along the south coast of the island to Port Erin and another to the west coast town of Peel. The trains were conveniently timed so you could travel on both the same day. Winter services on the St. John's to Ramsey line, once owned by the Manx Northern Railway, had by then been withdrawn completely.

My request for a holiday runabout ticket so early in the year was treated by the Douglas

14

booking clerk as a whim of one of these mad enthusiasts, but by Tuesday lunchtime I had had my 12s 6d worth of travel.

Monday morning dawned foggy, as did most days that week. As I walked to Douglas station, the coastal fog siren booming out its warning to sailors, men on ladders were sticking up the new season's posters for the bus and train services, for both forms of transport shared the same management.

At the steam shed nothing stirred, but at 10am, with a roar and a cloud of exhaust, one of the ex-County Donegal railcars emerged, with its brother obediently in tow. But for more than an hour the other end of Douglas station had been a hive of activity. A never-ending stream of lorries was ferrying the inwards parcels and goods off the recently-arrived steamer from the mainland to the station.

A time-and-motion study man would have wept. Those parcels had been unloaded from the ship to a lorry, driven about half a mile to the station, then unloaded, booked in and loaded onto the train. On arrival at the destination station they would, as likely as not, be unloaded again to be put on yet another lorry for the final delivery! No wonder regular *commercial* services on the IMR had to stop!

Parcels for stations along the Peel line (Crosby, St. John's and Peel itself) were by now being loaded into one of the IMR grey "G" class vans standing at the stop blocks. The railcars backed gently onto it, coupled up and promptly at 10.25 we set out — the driver, the guard and yours truly, their solitary passenger.

Because it was a damp day, the driver had taken the precaution of walking along the platform, sprinkling sand on the rails, so we had little difficulty in starting. Our return from Peel was to prove this a wise move!

The outward journey was uneventful, though I wondered how much those crossing keepers along the line were paid for opening the gates twice daily in winter. Surely some

form of ungated level crossing could have been accepted by the island Parliament, Tynwald?

At St. John's, Station Master George Crellin, certainly the best-known character of the IMR (though now sadly deceased) came to meet our train as if it were a crack express, bustling from the booking office to the signal box, and on to the level crossing gates. At Peel, on the other hand, the huge station building seemed almost deserted.

The railcars backed out and into a siding to drop the van, and to shunt onto another already loaded and waiting in the goods shed. They could not run round in the normal way because the shunting neck was too short for two coaches! By the following year Douglas works had fitted a through brake pipe on one of the "G" vans and this was coupled permanently between the two railcars.

How pleased I was to be joined by a handful of passengers for my return to Douglas. Presumably they were taking advantage of the interchange arrangements whereby rail tickets could also be used for return on the bus, for there would be no train back to Peel that day.

By now the mist had turned to rain and as we climbed to St. John's the railcars slipped to a halt. The driver climbed down and gave the sandbox a hefty clout with a spanner. This evidently cleared the blockage and we were able to start off and crawl towards Douglas, where I was able to cast my eyes for the first time on one of those Beyer beauties — No 12 *Hutchinson*.

Fortunately the powers-that-be had decreed a solitary railcar was not powerful enough to pull its brother and a van over the gradients of the south line, and so they still steamed one of the 2-4-0Ts for the midday train to Port Erin and back.

Despite its inconvenient timing, a few passengers joined me in the two bogie coaches and we eventually set off, providing my first steam ride on the three foot gauge. I was amazed at the speeds attained at times — and

Top: Out of Douglas past a decidedly droopy junction signal comes IOMR No 11 *Maitland* with the 14·05 to Port Erin, in the south-west of the island, on June 14 1968. *G. D. King*

Top left: Three of the IOMR 2-4-0Ts, Nos 8 *Fenella,* 10 *G. M. Wood* and 12 *Hutchinson* were specially decorated for the 1967 re-opening of the Railway on Saturday June 3 and are seen here at the buffer stops at Douglas. *G. W. Morrison*

Centre left: As the 16·34 from Peel rolls into Douglas station on June 22 1968, the firemen of both No 10 *G. M. Wood* and No 11 *Maitland* swing out of their cabs ready to uncouple — an operation often completed before the train finally came to a stand. *G. D. King*

Bottom left: In recent years, spare locomotives have been exhibited at Douglas Station rather than simply left in the shed. Here, No 13 *Kissack* shunts a string of eight sister locomotives — including the solitary 0-6-0T *Caledonia* — back to the shed at the end of the day's operation on July 1 1971. *G. D. King*

at the rough ride. The diesels certainly had many advantages in that respect.

This journey passed uneventfully, except that on the return trip I was joined in my compartment by a Castletown teacher who, it transpired, used the train each day to go home to Douglas.

The rest of my holiday week was spent on the IMR, the Douglas horse trams and the Manx Electric line, where I bought a workman's contract ticket. This entitled me to seven trips from Douglas to Ramsey for 12s 6d and I found I could even fit in a trip

over much of the line after high tea. There was no fear of missing the last train back to Douglas, because the crew changed over wherever the two cars passed!

But fascinating as I found the MER, my heart lay with the steam railway and I vowed to return soon, as I did the following year, 1964, in July when they were operating the "early high season" timetable.

This provided a much busier scene. At St John's, where trains were divided and changed engines, one could see trains from Douglas, Peel and Ramsey arrive within a few minutes of each other — and leave together as well. Steam reigned almost supreme, with the diesel railcars relegated to a solitary return working along the Ramsey line to Kirk Michael (where the railway owned a pleasure park) during the afternoon. Even so, they were invariably packed with passengers and on one occasion a party of Irish nurses sang Irish airs at the top of their voices all the way back to Douglas, bringing back memories of the cars' early days on the County Donegal lines.

Sunday provided another spectacle on the IMR. The only trains of the day made the short run from Douglas along the Peel line to Kirk Braddan, where an open air church service is held.

By 1964 the IMR had this off to a fine art, using a solitary locomotive and the railcars. Two sets of coaches would be standing ready

17

in the Port Erin platforms at Douglas; early passengers would be ushered into the first, the locomotive coupled up and an early start made for Braddan, where the passengers would alight at the ground-level cinder platform. Then the train continued to Union Mills, the next station along the line, where there was a passing loop. The locomotive would run round its train and propel the coaches further along the line towards Peel before returning light engine to Douglas to pick up the now well-filled second train and take the passengers to Braddan. When it reached Union Mills, and while it was running round these coaches, the staff would shut up Douglas station and set out on the railcars, with any late passengers.

At Braddan the railcars waited ahead of the locomotive, which uncoupled and stood a little forward of its coaches, in accordance with IMR Rules and Regulations. The Station Master from Douglas would unlock the little wooden booking hut and put up poster boards by the road inviting passengers to return to Douglas by train for the princely sum of 6d.

After the open air service the railcars filled first and returned to Douglas. Then came the

first steam train; the locomotive came off its train without delay on arrival at Douglas and immediately returned to pick up the second rake of coaches. Finally, the railcars made another trip to Braddan to collect the station staff. By midday the trains had been put away and the whole of Douglas station was shut up as if no trains had run that day.

In 1964 the Braddan trains were well filled and even after allowing for paying the staff

Top left: Having arrived at the southerly terminus of the system, No 4 *Loch* rests outside Port Erin shed in the lunch hour on June 28 1971. *G. D. King*

Bottom left: The same day, the camera caught No 4 *Loch* astride the level crossing at Port Erin whilst shunting empty stock in readyness for its next working back to Douglas. *G. D. King*

Right: IOMR No 10 *G. M. Wood* waits in the leafy shade of Castletown loop with the 16·15 Port Erin-Douglas as the ex-County Donegal railcars approach on the 16·05 Douglas-Port Erin working on June 13 1968. *G. D. King*

Bottom: Past the smartly-painted crossing gates and into the platform at Port St. Mary rolls No 13 *Kissack* with the 10·15 from Douglas on June 28 1971. *G. D. King*

Top left: On a fine morning in August 1965, No 5 *Mona* clatters across Glen Mooar Viaduct with the 10·30 Douglas-Peel train. *S. Basnett*

Bottom left: Trains pass at St Johns: No 5 *Mona* waits with a train from Peel to Douglas as sister engine No 7 *Tynwald* runs in with a westbound train on July 22 1968. *C. M. Whitehouse*

Right: The graceful lines of the Guard's lookout frame No 5 *Mona* as it moves carefully up to its train at Ramsey before departure back to Douglas. *M. Dunnett*

Below: St. Johns station, junction of the Peel and Ramsey lines, as well as the defunct Foxdale branch, on June 20 1968. No 10 *G. M. Wood* is coupling up to the 16·34 Peel-Douglas, headed by No 12 *Hutchinson* ready to pilot it forward to Douglas. *G. D. King*

Bottom: With the Irish Sea as a backdrop, No 12 *Hutchinson* heads the 10·20 Douglas-Ramsey along the cliff-tops at Devils Elbow, on the west coast of the Island between St Germains and Kirk Michael on June 21 1968 *G. D. King*

overtime rates, they must have covered costs. In addition, this Sunday service must have acted as an advert for the whole line, for even if passengers returned from Braddan by bus or car they had seen the steam train and might well return later in the week for a longer trip. What a pity this short length of the Peel line could not have been retained, perhaps run by enthusiasts, for the Sunday Braddan trains.

My last holiday on the island under the old regime was in May 1965. By then economic pressures had over-ruled the misgivings about railcars on the Port Erin line, and they were rostered to operate the whole winter service, timetabled as one return trip a day each to Peel and Port Erin. But I arrived at Douglas to find the Peel service "temporarily suspended" for track work and only the south line, to Port Erin, operating.

Fortunately, however, they were preparing for the start of the season and by Thursday steam was in charge; I could conveniently spend my week with two days of diesels, two of electrics (on the MER) and two of steam. On my final day enthusiasts had hired the railcars and they made their first trip through to Ramsey.

At that time goods and parcels were still sent around the island by rail, with all the transhipping it involved; little did I or anyone else realise at the time that the end was so near. People were still talking about the IMR buying the West Clare line's diesel locomotives and renovating the track. But the red light was there — or rather the red buses, with their 70 seats, on the Port Erin route.

The 1965 winter service started as usual, but by November the Company announced temporary closure "for maintenance". The story since then has been one of continuing attempts to run the line for tourists. It is a complicated story to be told another time.

Since then I have returned twice; in 1968 I arrived just as the new container service flopped. I travelled all over the system that year — to Peel and Ramsey and on the first train to Port Erin. I even saw the sole 0-6-0T, No 15 *Caledonia*, in steam.

But to my mind light green engines and mock Victorian costumes are not the same. I am still happy to support them and would hate the system to close completely, but how glad I am that I saw the line under the old regime, when things were little different from those genuine Victorian days and steam still reigned even if, by then, not supreme.

Right: On the last stage of its run in from Douglas, a train picks its way through the creeks and backyards of Peel on July 22 1968. *M. Dunnett*

Sporting "special following in opposite direction" boards, No 12 canters through the rolling countryside west of St Johns with the 15·40 Douglas-Peel on June 20 1968. *G. D. King*

Home via Suez

Henry Stanton

Across the world, the crack expresses of today and the diesel and electric locomotives that haul them are often painted in distinctive liveries, and are externally well maintained and clean. But on the very same railways, the motive power and rolling stock diagrammed for the less glamorous duties often carries dull liveries and is generally dirty and unkempt.

The year 1914, when engine and carriage cleaners throughout the world were both cheap and plentiful, and before the austerities and economies of World War I and its after-match had taken their toll, saw a unique combination of the widest variety of locomotive and rolling stock liveries on the largest number of railways in the world. Ever since, railways have been merged or closed, and never again shall we see such varied liveries with such high standards of cleaning and maintenance, with special attention to paint and brasswork — of all engines and vehicles, not merely those working selected services. This, too, was the end of the greatest number of efficient steam locomotive and comfortable carriage designs before the final evolution of powerful 'standard' types of engine in the 1930s and 1940s, and the introduction of all-steel construction and air conditioning of passenger stock.

In eager expectation of a glimpse of a few of these glories overseas, not least of all in Britain itself, I embarked at Bombay for Liver-pool in the autumn of 1914. I had seen a good deal, at the age of six, of the idiosyncrasies of locomotive, carriage and wagon design on the Indian railways, to say nothing of the liveries and workings, for there had been long and entrancing train journeys between the railway centre where we lived, and the railheads for summer 'hill stations'. There were in 1914 some 16 Class 1 Indian railways, which between them worked a total of 22 broad (5ft 6in) and metre gauge main-line systems. Besides these there were several minor lines in princely States (known as Rajahs' Railways) and many small narrow-gauge and light railways. All these had their own fleets of locomotives, carriages and wagons. But that, as Kipling would say, 'is another story'.

In those days all British children in India could read by the time they were six, because avoidance of the midday sun favoured reading lessons and reading. Friends and relatives in England kept one well supplied with railway books and periodicals — including one journal that happily flourishes still today — and even if they did not, copies could usually be found at major railway bookstalls throughout India and included plates that were master-pieces of colour printing. Children's books were very well produced and great care was taken to ensure factual accuracy. The railway ABCs (to teach the alphabet, not the 'spotting' ABCs of today) were usually scrupulously correct in colouring and information, and proved invaluable in the light of later experience and reading. Other sources of pleasure and information on railways in many countries were coloured postcards (notably Raphael Tuck's) and cigarette cards, plus the travel literature issued by the various railways. That of the several Indian railways was often excellent, but regrettably my sometime sizeable collection has long since disappeared.

My last day in India included my only trip in that sub-continent in a non-corridor com-partment of British type, in a Bombay suburban train hauled by a 4-4-2T of the broad-gauge Bombay, Baroda & Central India Railway. This reminded me, after the exotic appointments of Indian main-line coaches, of local travel in England dimly remembered from two years earlier, when I was only four.

The white-painted matchboard-bodied sleeping cars of the 3ft 6in gauge Sudan Government Railway were the first vehicles we saw when a few days later we went ashore for half an hour in the intense heat and glare of Port Sudan. This was a return to the exotic; one was still 'east of Suez' railwaywise! Waiting patiently near the sleepers stood a graceful outside-cylindered Atlantic built by Robert Stephenson. I cannot remember its colour, but it had presumably arrived from Khartoum with an express, perhaps a boat train. Nearby, an 0-6-0 of unquestionably British design was shunting wagons.

This raises a question. Why are (or were!) British-designed steam engines so instantly recognisable even though there were such wide differences between the various designs? To the practised eye, the steam products of French, German, pre-1914 Austrian, Spanish, Swedish, Swiss and Japanese, let alone North American, designers were instantly recognisable as such, but only because they each had a distinctive appearance.

There was, however, a much greater variation between British designs, even within one region. The track gauge could contribute to the differences, of course, but was not the main reason; in Australia, for instance, the 4ft 8½in gauge engines of the New South Wales Railways differed greatly from those of the Victorian Railways of slightly wider (5ft 3in) gauge, yet all were recognisably Australian — and all basically British. The greater part of the steam engines of the South African (3ft 6in), Nigerian (3ft 6in), East African (metre), Sudan (3ft 6in) and Egyptian State (4ft 8½in) were nearly all British-designed — totally dissimilar and yet recognisably British. There were differences in British-designed and

British-built locomotives supplied to India (5ft 6in and metre gauge), to Ceylon (5ft 6in), Malaya (metre) and China (4ft 8½in). And apart from their basically British looks, it would be hard to find a family likeness in the engines built early in this century for the Shanghai-Nanking Railway; there were elegant 4-2-2s (perhaps the last "singles" to be built in the world), Indian-looking 4-4-0s with double cabs, and Atlantics that vaguely resembled other British products for Chinese railways. On the Argentine lines that derived their motive power from Britain there developed a special Anglo-Argentine trend in design. Indeed, this unmistakably British stamp could be traced through all British-designed engines for a century, until the virtual cessation of steam locomotive exports in the 1950s.

In Egypt, well on the way west, the railways, I was told, were more European, if not quite British in character. From the ship anchored off Suez a British-looking 0-6-0 in Indian-red livery with a brass dome could be seen leaving the little station near the mouth of the Canal for Suez Town with a string of six-wheel coaches that looked vaguely Continental, with prominent fittings in their roofs for oil, or perhaps gas, lamps; they dated, as I afterwards discovered, from the Anglo-French joint influence, before British industry and British management prevailed on the Egyptian State Railways in the 1880s. Beyond Ismailia, where the railway follows the canal bank to Port Said, we were overtaken by a Cairo-Port Said express, headed by a rather small-boilered 4-4-0 with outside frames and a weatherboard and canopy for a cab; it too had a burnished brass dome and was in the ESR red livery. Behind the tender came a French-looking van and then half-a-dozen maroon first and second class side-corridor bogie coaches with American-type clerestory roofs on either side of a white restaurant car of the Cie Internationale des Wagons-Lits. Rattling along behind the upper-class part of the train were arc-roofed third class bogies with open end platforms literally bursting with passengers. At Kantara there was no sign as yet of the big railway installation that was to grow up at Kantara East, across the Canal, as a base for the Palestine campaign and later the western terminus of the Palestine Railways line to Tel Aviv, Haifa and Jerusalem and, for a short period during and after World War II, to the Lebanon, Syria and Turkey via the now-closed coastal rail link which was built by British and Commonwealth railway troops.

Next day at Port Said the kindly ship's passenger who had volunteered as my bear-leader took me to see the station. The motive power on view consisted of passenger 4-4-0s and 0-6-0s of the type seen from the ship, all built, I seem to remember, by Robert Stephenson. I looked in vain for the ornate yellow-painted combined engine and saloon supplied by the same builders to the Khedive Ismail, but was told that it was preserved at Cairo. (Is it there today?) No railway picture book was complete without featuring it — and sometimes also Dugald Drummond's somewhat similar inspection unit with which he used to prowl around the London & South Western. Vestibuled side-corridor vehicles were rare in India in 1914 and the handsome, well-appointed first and second class coaches of the Cairo expresses were intriguing, as was the use of the French language in ESR timetables and notices.

Two days later I was called on deck to see a Straits of Messina train ferry laden with green Italian State (FS) passenger vehicles and covered goods wagons crossing ahead of us from Villa San Giovanni (to starboard) to Messina. At Villa one could see what looked like 0-8-0Ts shunting vehicles on and off the ferries and further north, a passenger train of bogie stock heading towards Reggio behind an FS outside-cylindered 2-6-0.

Marseilles proved to be a thrill: a main-line railway, and plenty of it, plus harbour lines that popped out, somewhat as on Merseyside, of tunnels through the rock. The delights of Marseilles St. Charles terminus were enhanced

by the climb up the monumental staircase which gave progressively better views over the city and port. Because of the war there was no boat train from the quayside at La Joliette and it was almost impossible for civilians to cross France to Britain; but there was plenty going on at St. Charles and along the quays. Shunting everywhere was in the charge of elderly outside-cylindered 0-8-0Ts of the Paris Lyons & Mediterranean Railway (PLM) which dominated Marseilles. Steam engines seen at Marseilles, all in the PLM medium green, included magnificent Pacifics, 4-6-0s (one with a four-wheel tender!) and an aged outside-cylindered 2-4-2 decked with assorted fittings and with a weatherboard bent back to form the cab!

PLM main-line coaching stock was painted in different colours according to class — firsts were black and maroon, seconds black and ochre, and thirds and vans green. Also much in evidence were sleeping and restaurant cars of the Wagons-Lits Co., all varnished teak and gold lettering which I could not decipher. Among the first class vehicles was one incorporating *lits-salon* compartments, which I was astonished to see contained three short couches close together in a row. There were long, four-wheel, vestibuled side-corridor firsts and seconds apparently of fairly recent construction, and a varied assortment of old four- and six-wheelers with quadrant-shaped (quarter-light) windows. Many of the covered and open freight wagons had a guard's lookout at the end, like a perched-up sentry box. The manual signalling, with its complex of discs and chequerboards, was utterly incomprehensible, and contrasted with the simple, basically British-type semaphore signalling employed in India, Egypt and, as far as I could see from the ship, Italy.

One morning we took a local train of clean but aged stock along the line towards Port de Bouc, west of Marseilles, which runs on a *corniche* along the cliffs, through tunnels and over viaducts. As we diverged from the main-line to Arles, Lyons and Paris, a southbound *rapide* hauled by a Pacific emerged from a tunnel whistling furiously (I distinctly remember it as a much shriller whistle than I was used to in India, where we would sleep through the whistling of goods trains which were halted outside our bungalow while the drivers tried to wake the signalman!) The tunnel was that of La Nerthe, three miles long. The acrid smell of *briquette* smoke mingled with that of hot brakes as the *rapide* was checked on the descent to St. Charles, and thick black smoke billowed out of the tunnel long after the express had passed.

In railway-less Gibraltar I had resigned myself to the inferior joys of visiting Rock apes and rainwater reservoirs, but there came the unexpected treat of a trip across the bay to Algeciras. The journey was by a decrepit paddle steamer flying an outsize Spanish flag as though cocking a snook at the Royal Navy and British possession of the Rock. The 5ft 6in gauge lines on the quay at Algeciras looked familiar after India, but it was surprising to see flat-roofed four-wheel passenger coaches and covered wagons whose bodies seemed broader than they were high. At Algeciras station the afternoon train was about to leave for Cordoba, or it might have been Bobadilla. Algeciras was the terminus of a branch of (I was told) the Andaluces Railway. The train we saw included a Wagons-Lits Co sleeper and through MZA (Madrid Zaragoza & Alicante Railway) coaches for Madrid, where they were due next morning. The *wagon-lits* was a broad-gauge version of what I had seen at Marseilles. All the other coaching stock, both the MZA corridor vehicles and the presumably Andaluces four-wheelers, was externally clean with much burnished brasswork including oil lamps on the end vehicles. The MZA coaches were certainly of varnished teak, but I cannot remember the livery of the others. Heading the train was a black 0-6-0 of apparently British design; I seem to recall that the buffer beam canted up slightly at each end, and was painted yellow, not red. Such a scene, I believe, was typical of southern Spain

for the next 20 years. The whole set-up at Algeciras seemed one-horse; although we did not visit the small engine shed, we saw no other motive power.

On a raw Sunday morning a week later we dropped anchor in the Mersey and were soon being ferried by tender to Liverpool Landing Stage. Passengers had been told that a boat train would run to Euston from the adjacent Riverside station, but an official of the London & North Western, clad in a frock coat and top hat, announced in a mournful voice that because of war exigencies the LNWR was unable to provide a boat train (although I doubt if there were enough of us to warrant one anyway) but had instead provided buses and taxis to take us to Lime Street, where there would be reserved compartments in the midday express. I did not know that the boat train would have afforded an exciting trip round sharp dockside curves and up through the tunnel to Edge Hill, with the special 0-4-2STs slipping perhaps in the tunnel; I only discovered I had been robbed of this treat later.

At Lime Street we found that both the Precursor heading our train and the variegated assemblage of LNWR corridor stock (LNWR expresses, apart from a few Anglo-Scottish and American Special services, were never uniform in composition) were grubby and unkempt, and the coaches were not properly boarded up — not even the American-roofed 12-wheel restaurant car with its baroque handrails, which I much admired.

The afternoon run to London proved tedious, even for me, and we lost time as darkness descended. Edge Hill, however, and the Runcorn Bridge, Weaver Junction and the approaches to Crewe were thrilling, as was Crewe station even on a wartime Sunday — though I was reluctant to believe that the red 0-6-2T and coaches I saw were not Midland but, as someone pointed out, the property of the North Stafford Railway. It was soon too misty and dark to see out and a tired six-year-old was fast asleep as we pulled into Euston.

Standards

Right: The only three-cylinder BR Standard engine to be built, Class 8P Pacific No 71000 *Duke of Gloucester* hurries past Basford Hall Junction with an Ian Allan "Trains Illustrated" excursion. Basically a "Super Britannia" with an additional cylinder, double chimney and Caprotti valve gear, the 'Duke' was built, on paper at least, to replace the ill-fated rebuilt turbomotive, *Princess Anne*, destroyed in the Harrow and Wealdstone disaster. But even its admirers wouldn't claim that it was the most successful of the BR designs and its work on the West Coast main line was, for the most part, unspectacular.

Bottom left: Despite the plethora of then still new Bulleid Pacifics, the Southern Region managed to acquire two Britannias for a while, and they were used on both the "Bournemouth Belle" and the "Golden Arrow". Ready at Stewarts Lane to work the latter, complete with special headboard and flags, is No 70004 *William Shakespear* on August 2 1955.   *N. Caplan*

on the Paddington-South Wales line, and it is on this route, at Newport, that we find a clean and tidy No 70025 *Western Star* ready to depart with the 07·50 Fishguard-Paddington. Like all the Western Region engines, *Western Star* was fitted with modified smoke deflectors without grab rails after sister engine *Polar Star* came to grief in the Didcot disaster.   *G. F. Heiron*

Above: The Britannias, on the other hand, seemed to be welcomed wherever they went — although some Western Region men could not get on with them at first — and at one time or another they worked on all six Regions of BR. They did sterling work in the early days

Bottom: That the Britannias, like all the Standard classes, were designed for accessibility and easy maintenance is underlined by this low angle view of the 70006 *Robert Burns* simmering gently on York shed on a warm night in August 1963.   *C. P. Walker*

Above: Although at one time in service on all six Regions of BR, in their later years all the Britannia Pacifics were concentrated on the LMR, and towards the end, nearly all were concentrated at Carlisle Kingmoor Shed, including No 70041 *Sir John Moore* seen here hurrying through the Lune Gorge on July 17 1965 with a Liverpool-Glasgow train. *Derek Cross*

Top left: Built largely as a result of the impressive performance of the Bulleid Light Pacifics on the Highland during the Locomotive Exchanges of 1948, the 'Clan' Pacifics were a lighter version of the Britannia. Ten were built, but a further order for 15 — including some, incredibly, for the Southern Region — was cancelled because of impending dieselisation. Naturally, the class spent most of its time in Scotland, although ironically they never worked on the Highland Main line with any regularity because of the large number of quite competent Stanier Class 5s which had by then become available. Visits to the North Midlands by both the Midland and North Western routes were not however, uncommon; here No 72007 *Clan Mackintosh* rolls into Hellifield, a little away from its usual haunts, with an RCTS rail tour on May 23 1964. *J. K. Morton*

Centre left: Later examples of the 251 BR Standard Class 9F 2-10-0s were built with double-chimneys, including No 92209 pictured here running into Bournemouth Central tender-first on March 8 1966 with an RCTS special and passing Britannia Pacific No 70020 *Mercury* — which later took the special back to Waterloo — in the shed yard. *A. Richardson*

Bottom left: Ten of the early Standard Class 9F 2-10-0s, Nos 92020-9, were experimentally built with Franco-Crosti boilers and preheaters in 1955, but the expected fuel savings did not materialise, while the unorthodox situation of the main chimney two-thirds of the way back along the boiler gave rise to vociferous complaints from half-suffocated crews, so all ten were modified for orthodox working in 1959 and the pre-heaters were subsequently removed. Here, still working Crosti-wise, No 92024 emerges from Knighton Tunnel, south of Leicester, with a train of limestone empties for Desborough on July 18 1958. *M. S. Taylor*

Left: In the last years of steam on BR, the 'Long Meg' anhydrite ore trains from Long Meg sidings on the Midland line between Carlisle and Appleby, up over Ais Gill to Widnes were probably the hardest — and bleakest — steam workings in the country. In typical Pennine weather, Class 9F 2-10-0 No 92009 blasts up the last few yards to Ais Gill Summit with a southbound 'Long Meg' on December 9 1967. *Allan Stewart*

Bottom: From 1957 onwards, both the Western and Southern Regions began to equip their Standard Class 4 4-6-0s with double chimneys, but whereas Swindon fitted a rather heavy and cumbersome-looking version, the Southern produced their own design which was shorter and altogether more handsome, as seen here on No 75075 as it stands among the ashes at Nine Elms on April 22 1967. *G. T. Robinson*

Top right: Apart from the 9F 2-10-0s, the most numerous of the other Standard engines were the Class 5 4-6-0s. Numbering 172 in all, they were to be seen on all Regions of BR and although they sported all the "Standard" features, they were nevertheless quite clearly direct descendents of the Stanier Class 5. On the Southern, they often showed following electric trains a clean pair of heels, both on the Kent Coast lines and, after electrification there, on the Western Section. It is on the latter that the camera caught No 73022 heading down the local line through the tree-lined St John's cutting west of Woking with a Sunday special on July 3 1966. *David Hill*

Bottom right: Although they achieved some quite spectacular feats on passenger trains, the 9Fs inevitably spent by far the majority of their time on heavy freight work. During one such task, single-chimney No 92061 pauses on the avoiding line at Newcastle Central to take water on a warm June day in 1966. *C. F. Burton*

Until closure in 1962, the steeply-graded and severely weight-restricted ex North-Eastern Railway line from Darlington through Barnard Castle and over Stainmore Summit to Penrith was the domain of the 20 Standard Class 3 Moguls. On the last day of services over the line, January 21 1962, Class 3 2-6-0 No 77003 pilots Class 4 2-6-0 No 76049 away from Darlington on the first leg of the RCTS 'Stainmore Limited' special to Penrith and Carlisle which, on its return, became the last train to work over the line.   *Colin T. Gifford*

Top: The BR Standard Class 4 4-6-0 was in reality a tender version of the Standard Class 4 2-6-4T, itself a development of the LMS Fairburn 2-6-4T. It was intended for use in those areas — such as Central Wales — where a larger working range than a tank could provide was called for, but where axle load restrictions precluded the use of the Class 5 engines. Inevitably, as time went by they were used elsewhere as well; certainly it was not for axle load restrictions that No 75030 was used on this permanent way train over Shap Summit on December 29 1967! *P. Weightman*

Bottom: Just as the BR Standard Class 5 4-6-0 was a direct descendant of the Stanier Class 5, so the Standard Class 4 2-6-0 was clearly derived from the LMS Ivatt Class 4 Mogul. Here both Standard versions — Class 4 2-6-0 No 76015 and Class 5 4-6-0 No 73050 — hurry through picturesque Midsomer Norton Station on the Somerset & Dorset line with an excursion from Bristol to Bournemouth on Whit Sunday June 5 1960. *Ivo Peters*

Above: In the same way, the BR Standard Class 2 2-6-0 had obvious family connections with the small Ivatt Moguls. In this shot of Newton Stewart on the now closed Dumfries-Stranraer line, Class 2 2-6-0 No 78016 waits quietly with the Whithorn branch goods for Class 4 2-6-0 No 76072 to depart with a two-coach train for Stranraer on May 22 1964. *Derek Cross*

Top right: The Standard Class 2 2-6-2T was, like its tender engine sisters, merely a Standard development of the Ivatt 'Mickey Mouse' 2-6-2Ts. But they found useful work on many of the byways of pre-Beeching British Railways, and sometimes on the main lines as well. Here No 84026 rolls into pre-electrification Ashford with a train from Margate via Canturbury to meet newly-rebuilt SR West Country Pacific No 34004 *Yeovil* blowing off impatiently at the head of a down extra to Deal.
Derek Cross

Centre right: Like their sister Class 3 2-6-0 tender engines, the Standard Class 3 2-6-2Ts did not rely completely on LMS practice, for their boilers were based upon the Swindon No 2 boiler, used on the GW 5100, 5600 and 8100 class tank engines. They too performed a useful range of tasks, often on cross country services, as was No 82002 here seen joining the main Somerset and Dorset line at Templecombe with a Templecombe-Highbridge train on June 28 1962. *Derek Cross*

Bottom right: The BR Standard Class 4 2-6-4Ts were as successful as their predecessors, the LMS Stanier and Fairburn engines, and performed a wide range of work throughout the system on everything from suburban passenger to freight and even, as here, banking duties. Class 4 2-6-4T No 80111 blackens the Dumfriesshire skies as it pounds through Greskine and up to Beattock Summit at the tail of a heavy northbound freight on June 17 1966. *Derek Cross*

The Cardiff Valleys Division

William Jones

Until the Grouping there was no Cardiff division of the GWR, such pre-1923 GWR lines as there were in the area coming under the Newport Division. But the number of small railways in the Cardiff area which came into the Great Western fold in 1923 was such that it was necessary to form a special Cardiff Valleys Division, with headquarters at the Queen Street Station of the former Taff Vale Railway at Cardiff. Other Railways totally embraced by the new division were the Rhymney, Barry, and Cardiff, while parts of the Brecon and Merthyr, Alexander Dock, and Rhondda and Swansea Bay lines all entered the division at various points.

These small Welsh lines were prosperous and carried prodigious volumes of traffic. The Taff Vale once paid a dividend of 17 per cent and the Barry never produced less than 10 per cent in its short 37 years of independent existence. The Rhymney carried a very heavy traffic in proportion to its modest mileage, and its main station in Cardiff also accommodated the trains of the youngest constituent of all, the ambitious Cardiff Railway which, dating only from 1911, constructed a main line parallel to the Taff Vale from Heath Junction on the Rhymney to Rhydyfelin, near Teforest, but failed to effect a workable junction at the latter point.

After amalgamation of the Welsh lines, and with their large Dock undertakings, the GWR claimed that it paid a tenth of the rates of the City of Cardiff! In fact, the ratable value of GWR property in Cardiff was considerably greater than that of any other city on the system, and the rates paid to Glamorganshire were higher than any others in a GWR-served county.

The Taff Vale was the first public railway in Wales, opened from Merthyr through Pontypridd to Cardiff in 1841. It was later extended from Pontypridd up the Rhondda Valley to Porth, Treherbert and Maerdy with other branches to Ynysybwl and Nelson, and a long branch southward to Llantrissant and Cowbridge reaching the sea at Aberthaw, where it was hoped to develop a port. The Taff Vale owned the Penarth Harbour Dock and Railway on the south side of Cardiff and the line was extended round the coast to Sully, eventually joining the Barry Railway near Cadoxton.

The locomotive works was at West Yard, Cardiff Docks, and the Carriage and Wagon Works at Cathays, which also boasted the largest running shed on the system. There were also sheds at Penarth Dock, Radyr, Coke Ovens (Pontypridd), Abercynon, Treherbert, Ferndale, Aberdare, and Merthyr (GWR), and smaller depots at Roath Branch and Cowbridge. There were 112 route miles, most of it double track, although it also included 22 miles of quadruple track in addition to freight lines around each side of Cardiff avoiding the main stations. Locomotive stock at Grouping totalled 275 units, 209 of which

Top: Sandwiched between auto-coaches, GW 6400 Class 0-6-0PT No 6431 sets out from Abercynon up the Taff Vale line with the 11·25 to Aberdare on August 3 1957. *S. Rickard*

Centre: GW 6400 Class 0-6-0PT No 6402 accelerates the 11·28 Machen-Pontypridd auto train away from Penrhos Junction, West of Caerphilly on the former · Rhymney Railway, on September 3, 1954. *S. Rickard*

Bottom: Rebuilt Taff Vale Railway Class A 0-6-2T No 367 approaches Heath Halt (High Level) at the head of the 18·15 Cardiff-Bargoed train on July 27 1953. *S. Rickard*

were 0-6-2Ts; the rest comprised 13 0-6-0Ts, six 4-4-2Ts, three 4-4-0Ts, two 0-4-0Ts and 42 0-6-0 tender engines. Most of the older engines had 17½in by 26in cylinders and 4ft 6½in coupled wheels, but some, including 15 class U 0-6-2Ts, had 5ft 3in wheels. The last engines to be built before grouping were a large batch of 58 handsome Class A 0-6-2Ts with 18½in by 26in cylinders and 5ft 3in coupled wheels, used mostly on passenger trains.

Main line trains included modern (for 1921!) elliptical roofed bogie coaches and six-wheel guard's vans. Trains ran alternately from Penarth or Bute Road (Cardiff Docks) through Cardiff and Pontypridd to Treherbert and Merthyr. The main train would consist of three or four bogie coaches and two six-wheeled vans, plus two older short bogie coaches and a six-wheel van forming portion detached at Porth for Maerdy, or at Abercynon for Aberdare. A number of Treherbert trains continued over the Rhondda and Swansea Bay Railway to Aberavon and Swansea and were formed of R&SB coaches, latterly worked by A Class 0-6-2Ts. There was also a frequent service from the Penarth line to Cardiff Clarence Road, serving the shipping and colliery office area. In business hours they were formed of 10 four-wheelers or five converted steam rail cars forming open saloons and were worked by class U or O3 0-6-2Ts. Push-pull auto trains were frequently used, formed of two or four cars, in the latter case with the engine, usually a 4-4-2T, 4-4-0T or small 0-6-2T, in the middle. Auto trains also worked most of the branches. Additional trains were run from the Valleys to Cardiff and the Penarth line at Bank Holidays and on miner's holidays, when an interesting set of coaches was often used comprising 10 four-wheelers, purchased second-hand from the Metropolitan District Railway after electrification of the latter had rendered them surplus. The Taff Vale coach livery was reddish brown and cream, and the engines lined black. The frequency of the mineral trains was a most impressive feature and for short hauls

from the storage sidings to the Docks, brake vans were often dispensed with, motive power being usually either the smaller-wheeled 0-6-2Ts or the 0-6-0 tender engines. The class V 0-6-0STs were used mainly for shunting at Penarth Docks, and at Grangetown on the harbour lines.

The Rhymney Railway reached Cardiff in 1858, using running powers over the Taff Vale from Walnut Tree Junction, Taffs Well, until its own direct line from Aber Junction, North of Caerphilly, through the 1 mile 181 yard long Caerphilly tunnel and Llanishen was opened in 1871. Route mileage was 51, which apart from the main line from Cardiff to Rhymney Bridge, the junction with the LNWR, included branches from Aber Junction, Caerphilly, to Senghenydd, and from Ystrad Mynach to the GWR Pontypool-Neath line at Hengoed. A short branch from Ystrad Mynach to the same line, further along at Penalltau Junction gave access to two branches jointly owned with the GWR — from Quakers Yard to Merthyr and from Nelson to Dowlais (Cae Harris). There was also a branch northward from Bargoed on the main line to Deri, where it made an end-on junction with the Brecon & Merthyr Railway. By using this branch and the spur from the Rhymney south of Bargoed station, the B&M ran a through service from Brecon to Newport. The Cylla branch was a short mineral line from Ystrad Mynach to Penalltau colliery.

A branch south east of Caerphilly gave access to the B&M branch from Machen and was used by the Pontypridd, Caerphilly and Newport trains of the Alexander (Newport and South Wales) Docks and Railway Co. These trains ran from the Taff Vale station at Pontypridd over their own line through the Treforest area before joining the Rhymney at Penrhos Junction on the Aber Junction-Walnut Tree Junction section. From Penrhos Junction a direct spur brought them into Caerphilly Station. It is interesting to note that the junction at Penrhos became even

Top: Along the Rhymney Valley through Llanbradach station towards the colliery comes GW 5700 Class 0-6-0PT No 7724 at the head of a short freight train on April 27 1957. *S. Rickard*

Below: Tonteg Junction on the former Barry Railway on October 25 1956 with GW 5600 Class 0-6-2T No 5680 heading an up coal train off the single line from Cwm Colliery towards Treforest. The disused direct line to Trehafod is on the left. *S. Rickard*

Penrhos Junction again, with GW 5600 Class 0-6-2T
No 5627 rattling past with the 12·25 Aber Junction-
Walnut Tree West freight on October 4 1957.
S. Rickard

more complicated when the Barry Railway
joined the Rhymney there in 1901, and from
then on there were extensive sidings all the
way between this point and Aber Junction.

In 1875 the London & North Western
Railway was granted running powers over
the entire length of the Rhymney main line to
Cardiff Docks, where it proceeded to establish
its own Goods station and 45 chains of its own
lines. Regular daily freight trains ran between
Abergavenny and Cardiff via Rhymney, and
the LNWR acted as goods cartage agents for
the Rhymney in the Cardiff area. So closely
did the Rhymney become tied to the LNWR
that it was a surprise when it was not absorbed
into the LMS at Grouping.

The Rhymney conveyed heavy mineral
traffic off all the lines mentioned and in addition contrived to obtain running powers over

the GWR from Quakers Yard to Middle Duf-
fryn in the Aberdare Valley, from which
point it ran mineral trains to Cardiff via
Ystrad Mynach in competition with the Taff
Vale. Most of the traffic went down to Car-
diff but some was handed to the Alexander
Dock at Caerphilly for onward transit to
Newport, to the Barry Railway at Penrhos,
or to the Taff Vale at Radyr for Penarth via
Walnut Tree Junction.

Main passenger services ran from Cardiff to
Rhymney Bridge and to Merthyr via Ystrad
Mynach and Quakers Yard, with connecting
branch services from Caerphilly to
Senghenydd and from Nelson to Dowlais.
The LNWR ran through trains over
Rhymney metals from Cardiff to North
Wales, Liverpool and Manchester. The Car-
diff station and head office of the company
was in The Parade while the main works was
at Cardiff Docks until more modern facilities
were provided at Caerphilly in 1902. Sheds
were provided at Cardiff (East Dock),
Crwys, Senghenydd, Taffs Well, Rhymney

tance express service in conjunction with the Great Western and Great Central Railways — from Barry to Newcastle-on-Tyne. The two larger companies provided the coaches and Barry locos simply worked it to and from Cardiff. The Works and main locomotive shed was at Barry, but there were also small sheds at Coity and Trehafod.

The first docks in Cardoff were opened in 1839 by the Marquis of Bute, and until about 1860 the Taff Vale provided locomotives to work the estate. After this time, the Marquis provided his own engines and in 1886 formed the Bute Docks Co. In 1897 the Cardiff Railway Company was formed to take over the Bute Docks Co and the former Marquis of Bute's Railway. It then turned its attention to the construction of a line up the Taff Valley from a junction with the Rhymney Railway at Heath, $3\frac{1}{4}$ miles from the Docks, to Rhydyfelin from which point it was intended to continue to a junction with the Taff Vale at Teforest, but as previously described in the event the Cardiff Railway failed to effect a workable junction. The line was opened on March 1 1911; freight traffic was meagre because the Company could not develop its line in competition with the Taff Vale as it originally intended.

With the completion of the Cardiff Railway, it was possible to take a cross-section of the Taff Valley about $1\frac{3}{4}$ miles south of Pontypridd and find railways running at six different levels. They were the Barry Tonteg-Trehafod and Tonteg-Treforest lines, the Taff Vale Llantrissant and Taff's Well lines, the Pontypridd-Caerphilly line of the Alexander Dock and Railway Co, and the new Cardiff Railway line.

The main works of the Cardiff Railway was at Tyndall Street and the running shed at East Moors Road. There were 35 locomotives, 13 of which were Kitson 0-6-2Ts similar in design to the Taff Vale engines except that some had extended side tanks. In fact, three of the large 0-6-2Ts were almost identical with the Taff Vale O4 class. There were also 20 0-6-0 saddle or side tanks (including three ex-GWR Dean 1661 class) one 0-4-0T and one Webb 2-4-2T purchased from the LNWR named *Earl of Dumfries*. Two two-car rail motors with power units by Sissons of Gloucester worked the passenger service initially but the motor cars were later converted to trailers and the resultant two car sets hauled by one of the 0-6-0Ts or the 2-4-2T.

This then is a brief history of the major lines and an outline of their rolling stock at the time they were merged to form the new Cardiff Valleys Division of the GWR. The five years following Grouping was to prove an exciting and busy period but alas! few records now exist. The export coal traffic was returning to normal after the upheaval caused by the Great War and the passenger traffic kept to the same day-to-day pattern except for the introduction of some special workings such as Pontypool Road to Cardiff Parade via Crumlin, Hengoed Viaduct and the Rhymney line.

The first major change in the pattern of the passenger services came about following the rebuilding of Cardiff Queen St station in 1928 with two additional platforms to take Rhymney and Cardiff Railway trains, thus allowing the closure of Parade station. From then on Cardiff Railway trains from Rhydyfelin and Whitchurch were extended to Bute Road, in the heart of the shipping and colliery office district and, with the rapid housing development then taking place in the northern suburbs, this proved to be a popular service. Five and six coach trains had to be run in business hours to serve Whitchurch and Coryton, but beyond Coryton the line ran parallel to the Taff Vale line and the main road, on which bus services were by now developing, and the passenger service over this northerly section was withdrawn in 1931.

The Queen Street rebuilding also allowed one or two Rhymney trains to be extended to Bute Road and Penarth, and there were occasional workings from Barry onto the Taff Vale section, but basically the services retained much of their original pattern until after Nationalisation when the Timetable was completely recast with the introduction of an interval service in 1953.

The post-Grouping changes to the locomotive stock were most interesting but went largely unrecorded at the time. Most of the smaller engines that survived were eventually fitted with GWR chimneys and other boiler fittings, and some acquired Swindon parallel Belpaire boilers. The larger engines meanwhile received standard GWR taper boilers, except for a few Rhymney and Taff Vale O4 class 0-6-2Ts. All 58 of the Taff Vale As received new S1OKA superheated taper boilers with 200lb sq in pressure with a resultant marked improvement in performance, while a couple of the Barry 2-4-2Ts received large parallel Belpaire boilers with superheaters although they did not last much longer afterwards!

The longest survivors were the Taff Vale As, the last of which was withdrawn in August 1957, and the Rhymney R 0-6-2Ts, which survived unrebuilt until October 1957. The last Barry 0-6-2T went in 1951, but the same Company's 0-8-0s and 0-8-2Ts were early victims, as were the Taff Vale 0-6-0 tender engines and Rhymney saddle tanks, most of which were gone by 1930. Perhaps the biggest surprise was the early scrapping of the entire class of Barry L 0-6-4Ts, built in 1914 all of which were gone by 1926, in spite of being fitted with standard GWR taper boilers. Frequent bogie derailments were said to be the main reason, but undoubtedly the advent of the first of the 200 GWR standard 5600 Class 0-6-2Ts also influenced the decision. Built especially for the South Wales lines between 1925 and 1929 and based largely on the later Rhymney 0-6-2Ts, the new engines had 18½in by 26in cylinders, 4ft 7½in coupled wheels, 200lb sq in superheated boilers and were fitted with piston valves.

The GWR also introduced their 4200 class 2-8-0Ts in the valleys, but their long wheelbase gave trouble on sharp curves and their outside cylinders were tight for clearance in places. The ubiquitous 0-6-0PT was tried and proved very successful on the lighter jobs; no doubt spurred by this success, they were tried on the main Taff Vale passenger services but were quite obviously underpowered for such work and were soon withdrawn from it.

The Barry Railway already had two large GWR 5ft 8in 2-6-2Ts on loan at the time of Grouping, and had designed some similar engines themselves, using the boiler of their 0-6-4Ts and 4ft 7½in wheels, but the Grouping halted construction. The first change on the Cardiff-Barry service was the introduction of GWR 3600 2-4-2Ts with 5ft 2in wheels and, later, the 3900 class 2-6-2Ts with 5ft 2in wheels. Paradoxically, this service was eventually monopolised by the rebuilt Taff Vale As while the main Taff Vale services were handled by the new 5600 0-6-2Ts. On the Rhymney line the Barry B1, and the Taff Vale O2 and U1 class 0-6-2Ts were tried, but the services eventually became the province of the new 5600s, Rhymney AP (5ft 0in) 0-6-2Ts, some of which were rebuilt, and a few Taff As that also worked turns over their own system and odd trips from Aberdare out over the GWR Pontypool-Neath line.

In the early days after Grouping, some of the Cardiff line off-peak auto services were worked by Taff Vale 4-4-0Ts, 4-4-2Ts or even the 0-6-2Ts. In 1932 the GWR introduced new 6400 class 0-6-0PTs with 4ft 7½in wheels on all the auto services. Two years previously, the off-peak Penarth service had been the testing ground for the first 5ft 2in 5400 class 0-6-0PT No. 5400. The first outwardly visible alterations to the coaching stock after Grouping was repainting in GWR chocolate and cream livery, the sets of four- and six-wheeled coaches having "NOT TO RUN IN THROUGH FAST TRAINS" painted on their underframes at the same time. None of the four and six wheelers survived after 1930, by which time there had been an influx of the standard GWR 60ft steel-panelled coaches formed into two, four or five coach sets. However, some of the later Taff Vale and Barry bogie coaches remained in traffic until Nationalisation, as did a few Rhymney bogie coaches with wooden seats, used for miners trains until the general introduction of pit-head baths.

Two coach sets were added as branch valley portions to main four or five coach Taff Vale trains, and on the intensive Cardiff-Barry service the new five coach sets were used, plus a Rhymney bogie wooden-seater on weekdays for the use of the coal trimmers working at Barry Docks.

The GWR introduced a couple of express services in the Cardiff Valleys Area in the 1920s. The first was a through train to Aberystwyth with corridor coaches and roof boards proclaiming "Cardiff (Parade), Caerphilly, Treherbert, Carmarthen and Aberystwyth", while the second, three coaches only but also suitably lettered, ran from Barry to Llandrindod Wells. Neither service lasted long, for the main passenger business was from the Valleys down to Cardiff and the coast, and it was this that continued to flourish. A substantial passenger service was maintained right through the Second World War due to the importance to the war effort of the mining, iron and steel and general manufacturing activity of South Wales. A number of interesting workers specials were run daily from the Valleys to the Royal Ordnance Factories at Tremains, near Bridgend, and Glascoed, on the Pontypool Road-Usk line. There were also non-stop relief trains from Pontypridd to Cardiff General direct via Radyr and the Waterhall Loop Line, and some extra Cardiff-Barry Island trains non-stop between Grangetown and Barry, apparently to encourage "holidays at home!"

After Grouping, the GWR developed excursion traffic to Barry Island from all parts of the system. Barry Island station was enlarged and return excursions were to be seen departing at about five-minute intervals on summer Sunday and Bank Holiday evenings. Most of the excursions from the Valleys were hauled by 5600 class 0-6-2Ts or, later, the 4100 class 2-6-2Ts, while the longer distance trains were brought in by 4300 class 2-6-0s and Hall, Grange, and Castle class 4-6-0s. Two regular Sunday excursions from the LMS Sirhowy Valley line were for many years hauled by LNWR "Super D" 0-8-0s. The latter and the 4300 class were permitted to turn by running round Barry Dock, but the 4-6-0s had to run light to Canton to turn, as also did the Britannia class Pacifics on their occasional visits. In the last years of steam operation, the growth of banana traffic through Barry brought a variety of 4-6-0s on the scene to work the trains including Halls, Castles and LMR Class 5, 6 and 7 4-6-0s.

Over the years, the changes on the civil engineering side no less interesting. The first major work was the enlargement of the ex-Taff Vale Queen Street station in 1928, as already mentioned. The main platforms were lengthened, the down platform being converted to an island, while another was added on the east side to provide two platforms for the ex-Rhymney and Cardiff Railway services, so permitting these trains to be extended to Bute Road (Docks), Cardiff General, and the coast. A spectacular double track scissors crossing had to be provided at the north end of the station to allow Taff Vale and Rhymney services access to all platforms. This was prefabricated and towed into position on a Sunday by two 2-8-0Ts. At the same time, a number of small signal boxes were closed and replaced by two new boxes, Cardiff Queen Street North and Cardiff Queen Street South, the former becoming the largest box in Wales at the time.

In 1926, the Rhymney Works at Caerphilly was rebuilt and enlarged to become the main locomotive works for all the South Wales lines, thus permitting closure of the Taff Vale works at West Yard, Bute Street. West Yard was a very restricted site, bounded by the Glamorganshire Canal on one side and Bute

Street on the other, with tracks at right angles to the main line. Access was by means of turn-tables and the tracks crossed the electric tram tracks in Bute Street, on which all traffic was halted while engines were being moved. After closure, the Taff Vale Goods shed nearby was demolished along with the redundant turn-tables, allowing Bute Road station to be rebuilt with two long platforms. The enlarged Caerphilly Works was capable of dealing with the repair of all the tank engines of the South Wales lines plus, latterly, a large number of larger tender engines including all the main ex-GWR classes, and BR Standard engines, including one Britannia Pacific and numerous class 9F 2-10-0s. Compared with the throughput in Rhymney days, the annual number of engines dealt with was quadrupled by the 1930s. In addition, over 100 engines from constituent companies had been rebuilt at Caerphilly with standard GWR boilers by 1949. Alas, this fine Works was closed in 1963, and instead a new Diesel Maintenance Depot was opened on the site of Canton shed at Cardiff, itself closed to steam in 1962, its engines being temporarily transferred to Cardiff East Dock. The new depot is capable of dealing with the maintenance requirements of all the diesel units in the Cardiff Division, which then extended west from Beachley Junction, Chepstow and south from Craven Arms to Fishguard and Aberystwyth, including the whole of South Wales.

Barry Island Station was enlarged in the late 1920s by lengthening both platforms and converting the down platform to an island. Also on the ex-Barry system, a new halt was built at Llandow, Wick Road, and another on the Cardiff Railway at Birchgrove, while platforms were lengthened at Heath and Rhiwbina Halts to take the longer peak hour trains. On the debit side, branch closures in the first decade of grouping included the ex-Taff Vale Aberthaw branch beyond Cowbridge in 1930 and the Nelson branch beyond Albion Colliery in 1932. The junction with the Llantrissant-Cowbridge branch at Maesmawr

was closed and the branch connected instead to the ex-Barry main line at Tonteg, utilising the Barry-Taff Vale connection thence to Treforest. At the same time, Barry line passenger trains between Tonteg and Trehafod were diverted onto the Taff Vale line at Treforest and the trains terminated at Pontypridd (Central), connecting with Taff Vale line trains on to Trehafod. This allowed the closure of the ex-Barry stations at Treforest and Pontypridd (Graig), and thereafter the Barry Tonteg-Trehafod line gradually fell into disuse, as it included the long Pontypridd tunnel which was expensive to maintain. The line was used at the latter end of the Second World War for the storage of large numbers of American Austerity 2-8-0s prior to D-day and was finally closed to all traffic in 1956. The ex-Barry connection between Penrhos Junction, near Caerphilly and Barry Junction on the Brecon & Merthyr line was closed and the large viaducts carrying the line over the Aber and Rhymney Valleys were dismantled in 1937. This was sensible rationalisation of former competing services, and in all these cases traffic could be conveniently diverted onto the other parallel routes without much inconvenience to passengers. There were no further closures until after Nationalisation.

In 1953, when the whole of the Cardiff Valleys timetable was completely recast, the Taff Vale and Barry services were merged and there was a basic half-hourly service from Barry Island through Cardiff to Pontypridd with alternate trains continuing hourly to either Treherbert or Merthyr. There were a number of additional trains at peak hours to and from Bute Road or Penarth, and there were seven trains between Queen Street and Pontypridd in the period 4.52 to 6.06pm — two to Merthyr (one a non-stop), three to Treherbert, and one each to Aberdare and Maerdy. In roughly the same period five Rhymney and three Coryton trains left the north end of Queen Street alone. Rhymney line trains were generally hourly throughout

to be frozen, it did not follow that this solidification took place in the interval of some six minutes (6.46 to 6.52pm) during which the points were bolted reversed to allow the passenger train to reach the platform, though it may have done so. It was possible, he said, that the accumulation and freezing was gradual, and that a few stones, disturbed perhaps by the passenger train, sufficed to prevent the subsequent full movement of the rocking shaft lever, and that it subsequently froze in that position.

Although this incident, the first in the chain of events leading to the accident, was due to extreme mischance, he felt the arrangement of the rocking shaft lever, with the end moving at so low a level, was not satisfactory.

He thought that the use of rocking arms of the type in use at Lichfield should be avoided except where they were strictly necessary, such as when a facing point lock lifting bar lies in the space between a check rail and the running rail. In the majority of cases where there were no check rails — and there were none at Lichfield — the use of a horizontal "scale beam" lever working entirely above the sleepers, with one end coupled to the lifting bar and the other to the drive-rod of the bolt, appeared to be preferable. This arrangement was in common use and did away with the need for special attention to the ballast level round the rocking shaft.

He attached no blame to Signalman Williams' failure to notice the incorrect action of the bolt, nor did he criticise him for using some force to restore lever No. 33 to normal, involving as it did the movement of some 200yd of rodding with an inertia approaching a ton. He was, however, critical of Williams' failure to observe whether signal No. 4 obeyed the lever movement when he "pulled off" for the fish train. Had he done so and discovered that it had not responded, regulations relating to defective signals would almost certainly have led to the discovery of the incorrect point setting, and would certainly have caused the fish train to be checked. In either event, the disaster would have been averted.

Commenting on the buckled down rod, the Inspecting Officer said that he considered the real fault to be in the arrangement of the down rod. He thought that an offset of more than 3in in the rodding between a pair of supports was generally undesirable. The reason for the increased offset was the use of LMSR 12in pedestal cranks, in place of the standard 9in cranks of the LNWR Webb variety frames. Despite this change, no additional restraint on the down rod was provided.

Having heard all the evidence, Lieut-Colonel Woodhouse finally concluded that, despite the evidence of witnesses to the contrary, signal No. 4 was probably at danger.

"A review of all the circumstances leads me to attach more weight to the tangible evidence than to the witnesses' recollection. Consequently I have formed the opinion that in all probability the Up Fast home signal, No. 4 remained at Danger at the material time and that Driver Read failed to observe and obey its indication. If this was so, he must share responsibility for the accident, but there are extenuating circumstances".

Lieut-Colonel Woodhouse dismissed at length the witnesses' evidence on the position of No. 4 signal, concluding that their statements were made mainly as a result of "auto-suggestion".

Like a Court of Law, this was the admission of circumstantial evidence as opposed to proof positive, but it must be noted that one small word occurs in his summing up — "If".

But, like Grantham, Shrewsbury and Salisbury, Lichfield will go down in railway history as a mystery. Was No. 4 signal held at "Danger" by the detector mechanism, or was it, by some quirk of fate, as Driver Read claimed, showing a "good green light all the time"?

The East Coast 'non-stop'

David Percival

Probably no other train demanded quite so much from the steam locomotive as did the East Coast 'non-stop'. This was the summer season express — or, to be precise, several named expresses over the years — which ran the 393 miles each weekday without a stop between Kings Cross and Edinburgh Waverley. Its history encompasses slightly more than 33 years, from May 1928 until September 1961, and is one of the success stories of the LNER Chief Mechanical Engineer Sir Nigel Gresley.

The beginnings of the story can be traced back to 1862, when the companies operating the East Coast Route began running a daily express at 10.00 from Kings Cross to Edinburgh. Apart from a brief period during the first world war, when it departed at 9.30, a 10.00 Edinburgh express has left Kings Cross on weekdays ever since, and the corresponding southbound train has the same record. The train was variously known as the 'Special Scotch Express', 'Flying Scotch Express' and 'Flying Scotchman' down the years, but it was not until after the Grouping of 1923 that the now-famous title 'Flying Scotsman' was officially adopted.

As a background to the period of non-stop running, it is interesting to recall the rivalry which existed between the companies operating the East and West Coast Routes from London to Scotland. In the 1860s, the

East Coast express took $10\frac{1}{2}$ hours on its journey and among its stops was one of half an hour at York for lunch, since there were no restaurant cars in those days. The up train, for some reason, took an hour longer! New, more direct, routes were opened in the North East during the next decade, resulting in an acceleration to nine hours by 1876.

From November 1887, third class passengers were admitted to the train (which, unlike its West Coast rival which ran from Euston to Glasgow and Edinburgh, had until then been restricted to first and second class accommodation) and this action led to the "Race to Edinburgh" of the following summer. Finding that they were losing third class traffic, the West Coast companies cut the schedule of the Edinburgh portion of their 10 o'clock express from ten to nine hours in June 1888. The reply from the East Coast companies was an acceleration to $8\frac{1}{2}$ hours in July. When the West Coast followed suit on August 1 (announcing their intention a few days in advance) the train from Kings Cross rather more than coincidentally reached Edinburgh in eight hours on the very same day! Again the West Coast timing was pared by 30 minutes, to which the East Coast retorted with a further cut, to $7\frac{3}{4}$ hours. So the West Coast made a supreme effort and reached Edinburgh in 7hr 38min — only to be beaten by a record 7hr $26\frac{3}{4}$min run (including a $26\frac{1}{2}$min stop at York) by the rival East Coast down train on the last day of August!

Timings on both routes were then settled by agreement at $8\frac{1}{2}$ hours. By the turn of the century, following the introduction of restaurant cars, a further cut to $8\frac{1}{4}$ hours was made by both sides, who agreed to maintain this timing for the Edinburgh daytime services. There the matter rested for over two decades, despite the development by the companies of both routes of larger and more powerful locomotives capable of hauling much heavier trains at faster average speeds.

Not until the mid-1920s, in the aftermath of Grouping, did a new form of competition

Top: Between platforms thronged with sightseers, the then LNER Class A1 Pacific No 4472 *Flying Scotsman* pulls out of Kings Cross with the inaugural non-stop northbound 'Flying Scotsman' on May 1, 1928. Curiously, this first train did not carry a headboard, although the Edinburgh Haymarket locomotive on the balancing southbound working did so; as soon as this became apparent, King's Cross depot, not to be outdone, quickly made another for their own locomotives to use!

Bottom: Just to prove they could do it as well, and no doubt to steal some of the thunder from the LNER, the LMS organised a special non-stop run from Euston to Glasgow on April 27 1928, just a week before the LNER were due to commence regular non-stop working to Edinburgh. For this piece of bravado, the LMS temporarily fitted Royal Scot Class 4-6-0 No 6113 *Cameronian* with a high-capacity tender with additional coal rails, as can be seen in this view of the special topping the summit of Beattock bank. *LPC Collection*

arise between the railways of Britain, particularly between the LMS (on the west coast) and the London & North Eastern Railway (on the east coast line). Long runs without intermediate stops for locomotive purposes were now quite possible. The LMS bestowed the title 'Royal Scot' on their 10.00 train to the north in June 1927, running it non-stop over the 236 miles between Euston and Carnforth, usually double-headed by a 'George the Fifth' 4-4-0 and a 'Claughton' 4-6-0. Now equipped with new Gresley Pacifics, the LNER in the following month gave the 'Flying Scotsman' a non-stop schedule between Kings Cross and Newcastle — a distance of 268 miles. But the LMS were beginning to take delivery of their new 'Royal Scot' 4-6-0s, and in September were able to dispense with the Carnforth stop and recapture the lead by changing engines on the down 'Royal Scot' just north of Carlisle, at Kingmoor, 301 miles from Euston.

Then came the summer of 1928. Nigel Gresley was not to be outdone by the West Coast people and designed a novel type of tender which incorporated a side corridor and gangway, so that crews could make their way from the footplate to the train and vice versa while the train was in motion. Thus it became possible to run non-stop over the 393 miles between Kings Cross and Edinburgh, with two sets of footplatemen sharing the duty.

The plan was devised under a cloak of secrecy, but an amusing anecdote in F. A. S. Brown's book on Gresley shows that LNER railwaymen, at least, had some idea of what was afoot. To avoid suspicion, the first of the new tenders was innocently attached to an Ivatt Atlantic at Doncaster Works for test. Not far from Doncaster, a signal halted the run beside an out-of-the-way signalbox. As the signalman came down the steps the driver complained that he had been assured of a clear road. The signalman replied that the road was indeed clear — but he had halted the special to look at the corridor tender!

The first batch of tenders was attached to ten of Gresley's Pacifics; two had by now been rebuilt with 220lb/sq in boilers and reclassified A3, while the remainder were the original A1s, with pressure of 180lb/sq in.

New 13-coach trains were provided for the 1928 'Flying Scotsman', although the stock

Right: The Royal Border Bridge at Berwick with A4 class 4-6-2 No 4492 *Dominion of New Zealand* crossing at the head of the down non-stop 'Flying Scotsman' in the summer of 1937. *LPC Collection*

Below: When the East Coast Main Line was closed by flood damage north of Berwick in July 1948, many main line trains, including the 'Flying Scotsman' were diverted via Leeds and the Midland main line over Ais Gill to Carlisle. The down train is seen here at Bell Busk, between Skipton and Hellifield in the charge of A4 class 4-6-2 No 25 *Falcon* one day in August. *W. Hubert Foster*

then in use was itself only four years old. Since passengers were to be confined to the train for more than eight hours, pleasant surroundings and special features were provided. The first class car of the triplet restaurant car unit was furnished in Louis XIV style, with loose armchairs, curtains and concealed lighting, and the third (now second) class diner was also attractively designed, though in a less elaborate style. A newsboy, selling newspapers and magazines, travelled in the train and a hairdressing saloon was built into one of the coaches, followed by a small cocktail bar in 1932.

So the 'non-stop' began as the 'Flying Scotsman', booked to run without a stop in each direction from the beginning of May 1928. The 'Royal Scot' was obliged to stop at Symington to split or join the Glasgow and Edinburgh portions, so a longer non-stop run was out of the question, and it continued to change engines at Carlisle. However, the LMS were not to be this easily upstaged, and cheekily stole a little of the limelight on the Friday before the LNER commenced non-stop running. On this day the northbound 'Royal Scot' was run as two separate trains; 'Royal Scot' 4-6-0 No. 6113 *Cameronian* took the Glasgow coaches without a stop over the 401½ miles from Euston, while Midland Compound 4-4-0 No. 1054 ran non-stop to Edinburgh — a distance of almost 400 miles.

The next attempt at non-stop running on the West Coast route did not come about until eight years later when, in the autumn before the LMS introduced their streamlined 'Coronation Scot' express, Stanier 'Princess Royal' Pacific No. 6201 *Princess Elizabeth* hauled a seven-coach test train non-stop from Euston to Glasgow in 5hr 53½min in November, 1936. Even more remarkable was the return trip next day, again non-stop and this time in adverse weather conditions. Hauling eight coaches, No. 6201 completed the journey in a time of 5hr 44¼min — 1½ hours less than the fastest Anglo-Scottish expresses of the day, and only three quarters of an hour more than today's electric services!

Returning to the events of 1928, on Tuesday May 1, crowds gathered at Kings Cross to see the departure of the first non-stop 'Flying Scotsman'. Suitably hauled by No. 4472, the A1 Pacific bearing the same name, the train carried pressmen, guests and Gresleyd himself, who conducted visitors through the tender to the footplate. Arrival at Waverley station was 12 minutes before time, while A3 No. 2580 *Shotover* brought the up train into Kings Cross 2½ minutes early. During that summer, both of these engines played a major part in the workings, each completing over 50 Monday-Saturday non-stop runs.

Because of the agreement on schedules, the 'Scotsman' — running non-stop during the

With its chime whistle protesting at adverse signals, A4 Class 4-6-2 No 60009 *Union of South Africa* slows the up "Elizabethan" into Peterborough North on September 4, 1954. *P. H. Wells*

peak summer months only — was restricted to an average speed of only 47.6mph. The following relief train made all the usual stops and still managed to achieve the same 8¼-hour timing! By 1932, however, express train speeds throughout the country had increased to such an extent that the LMS and LNER were forced to abandon the agreement .

The responsibility for supplying motive power was shared by Kings Cross and Haymarket depots, and remained so until the end of non-stop running; Pacifics from one depot hauled the down train and from the other the up train on alternate days. Before the war, Kings Cross and Gateshead crews manned the Kings Cross engine, while the Haymarket Pacific was handled by Haymarket and Kings Cross men. The crew on duty for the second part of the journey travelled in a reserved compartment at the front of the train and made their way to the footplate at Tollerton, a few miles north of York. Haymarket drivers had to refresh their knowledge of the route between there and Newcastle, which was otherwise the southerly limit of their normal duties. The rostered locomotives also worked corresponding trains on Sundays and, while Haymarket kept one engine on the duty for a fortnight or more, Kings Cross used two Pacifics, working alternate out-and-back trips.

An exception to the usual Pacific haulage occurred at the end of July 1930, when the experimental water-tube boilered 4-6-4 No. 10000 was employed for a brief spell.

The first four of Gresley's streamlined A4 Pacifics were completed in 1935 and almost immediately entered service on the newly-introduced 'Silver Jubilee' express. When the second batch of A4s appeared in 1936/7 some were available for general use on East Coast expresses, including the 'Scotsman'. All were paired with corridor tenders, ten of them taking the original variety built in 1928, thus ending the reign of the A3s on the 'non-stop'. By 1937 the summer train was running to a seven hour schedule, and the task of the A4s was made even more exacting in the following year by the introduction of a new set of coaching stock. Equipped with pressure-ventilation equipment, the 12-coach summer formation weighed 426 tons. A notable feature of the 1938 'Scotsman' stock was the

rebuilds, No. 60503 *Lord President* and at least five more V2s arrived at Kings Cross with up trains during 1958/9. One of the V2s passed Stevenage on time with the 'Elizabethan', indicating a swift change-over and subsequent fine running by the mixed traffic locomotive.

In each of the final two years there was only one failure en route, the occasion in 1961 being when No. 60030 *Golden Fleece* was replaced on the down 'Elizabethan' by A3 No. 60040 *Cameronian* at Newcastle on August 31. Curiously, the A4 was able to return south less than three hours later with the fast 17.00 Newcastle-Kings Cross.

The final chapter of non-stop working ended on Friday September 8, 1961, when the last down 'non-stop' was entrusted to No. 60022 *Mallard,* while the up train was hauled by No. 60009 *Union of South Africa.* Edinburgh and Kings Cross arrivals were, respectively, on time and two minutes early.

The summer relief to the 'Flying Scotsman' retained the name 'Elizabethan' for one more year, but was hauled by the new Class 55 'Deltic' diesels and, conforming with the general speed-up of 1962, was given a six-hour schedule. In spite of rumours that the off-duty crew would travel in the locomotive's rear cab, or that the Deltics were to be fitted with gangway connections, neither of these eventualities came about, and although 'The Elizabethan' was shown in the public timetable as a non-stop express, it in fact paused momentarily outside Newcastle to change crews. After only four weeks, however, this became an advertised stop at Newcastle.

But the story does not quite end with the introduction of diesel power. On June 2, 1962, the Stephenson Locomotive Society and Railway Correspondence & Travel Society jointly organised a Kings Cross-Aberdeen special which was to run non-stop to Edinburgh, hauled by *Mallard.* Unfortunately, a hot-box on a preceding freight train put paid to the attempt and the 'Aberdeen Flyer' was halted by signals a few miles south of Berwick.

There is just one more postscript to the story — and this, too, nearly ended in failure twice during the journey. May 1, 1968 was the fortieth anniversary of the first non-stop 'Flying Scotsman' and the preserved A3, No. 4472 *Flying Scotsman,* then owned by Alan Pegler, was scheduled to repeat its performance of 40 years earlier. Watched by an enormous crowd, the special departed from Kings Cross at 10.00 alongside the Deltic-hauled 'Flying Scotsman'. Pulling away first, it was overtaken by No. D9021 between the tunnels outside the terminus, where the two trains provided a splendid spectacle for 40 or more photographers and onlookers gathered in the vicinity. *Flying Scotsman* followed the regular express down the main line from Finsbury Park and things ran smoothly until a broken rail almost halted the special between Doncaster and York. Although No. 4472 was coupled to two tenders, and three water troughs were still in use on the northern part of the line, facilities were laid on for supplying water if necessary at Berwick. Because of two poor pick-ups, there was less water in the tenders than had been anticipated when the special approached the Border town, and a difficult decision had to be taken. It was decided to press on, but the train was diverted onto the goods line all the same and, with a signal at danger ahead, a tense few minutes passed as speed came down to a crawl. But the signal cleared, and the special continued to complete the run without a stop.

Flying Scotsman's achievement that day was a fine tribute to three decades of a very special kind of steam locomotive working and express train running. The 'non-stop' demanded — and received, from all grades of railwaymen on the East Coast — high standards of design, maintenance and operating skills.

Daisies, Bongols and Peacocks

Andrew Turk

Have you ever secretly wished you could gain some practical footplate experience, even though you might not care for a full-time railway career? Most of us dream about it, but very few people have tried it.

In 1971 I decided to break out of a rut, and that is how I came to apply for a job as fireman on the South African Railways, having been attracted by the reports, and film shows, given by recent visitors to the SAR.

The thick red tape took some time to cut, and I eventually arrived in Johannesburg in November 1971, only to discover that the red tape had been mostly red herring, and that such formalities as were necessary could easily have been completed within a week of my arrival in South Africa. Given free choice of allocation to any SAR depot, I plumped for Germiston — a mistake, as I shall explain later! But at the time Germiston seemed convenient, with an allocation of over 100 locomotives and situated between, and within easy reach of, Johannesburg and Pretoria. Another important factor was the short three-minute walk from the staff hostel to the shed!

Within 48 hours of leaving my Surrey home, I was climbing onto the footplate of No. 1524, a North British-built Belpaire-boilered 12A 4-8-2 built in 1920, to start my three-week practical training as "third man". It wasn't long before I had convinced the regular fireman that I knew the ropes,

whereupon he happily retired to the comfort of a nearby shunters' cabin! These three weeks were mostly spent shunting and even after a further fortnight behind a desk brushing up on regulations and signalling, I had still not realised that 90 per cent of the work at Germiston was shunting! By the time I passed out after five weeks (and no self-respecting enthusiast could fail to score at least 95 per cent in the passing-out tests!) I was fairly itching to get out on the main line.

Unfortunately it was not to be. I was allocated to a regular driver who had only been driving a year, and while we got on well together, we were stuck on the shunting link, which allows only about one week in ten out on the main line, and then only on inter-yard haulers — trip work in English. This was far from my idea of practical footplate experience, and I decided to apply for a transfer as soon as possible. Two possibilities were open to me — a Free State or Karroo depot, with large mechanically-fired 4-8-2 and 4-8-4 types, running heavy traffic on fast main lines, though with a total lack of scenic attraction and no fixed links, crews working on the "first in, first out" basis, or alternatively a depot in a more mountainous area such as the Cape or Natal, preferably with plenty of Garratts, and whose locals would be more likely to speak English then in the Free State where Afrikaans is the predominant language. I questioned Germiston men who had spent time at other depots and soon learnt that a popular shed for the Drivers was Masons Mill, Pietermaritzburg, though the firemen were not so sure — "too much work with bad Natal coal and cleaning heavily clinkered fires", they said. This however seemed to be the right place, with a pleasant climate, in an English-speaking area with superb scenery and mountainous lines with a high proportion of "road" work, and, last but not least, some 100 or so Garratt engines on the allocation.

In the event, my transfer took five months to arrange, giving me time to try my hand on all the different classes at Germiston, and on

Top: Beneath a pall of black smoke, South African Railways 15F Class 4-8-2 No 3074 swings round the curve at Karee Coppice on October 21 1971 with a freight from Bloemfontein. *K. Smith*

Bottom: Coasting into Idutywa in the Transkei comes SAR Class 14 CRB 4-8-2 No 1899 with an East London-Umtata train on August 10 1970. *L. A. Nixon*

all types of work, though mainly shunting. All three 0-8-0 S (for shunt) classes are represented there, of which the massive S1 took my fancy. With a grate larger than that of a Bulleid Pacific, they need very careful firing to avoid clinkering early during the regular 12-hour shifts. Germiston's coal is supplied by the Witbank coalfield and compared with British coal leaves much to be desired, but compared with Natal coal, as I was later to discover, it is excellent! The original S class shunters, built by Henschel in 1929, were definitely the black sheep at Germiston. Known as "Daisies", they are about the most uncomfortable engines I've ever ridden. Added to this, their tenders are totally inadequate, requiring the fireman to "trim" the coal after only three or four hours — something no fireman likes to do, least of all when shunting! Screw-type drop grates which would never drop and inaccessible injector steam valves were guaranteed to draw forth continual curses. Other engines for shunting duties were drawn from the large allocation of 12A/12AR, 15A/15AR, 15E and 15F 4-8-2s, plus a few 16CR 4-6-2s in their last year of life.

What work there was out on the main line would usually be handled by the hand-fired 15Es, with their enormous grates, far larger than any in British use.

The natives nicknamed them "Bongols", Bantu for donkey, though they are far from slow. Firemen had a ruder name for them — *Langpiel* is one way of referring to the long drive shaft to the rotary cam valves, but it can also be translated into a somewhat less fashionable meaning! Most are now withdrawn.

The Es were especially unpopular with drivers, due to the heavy manual action required to reverse the rotary-cam valvegear. On one occasion we were turning our E on the triangle outside Springs shed, prior to taking coal, and my mate, being in a hurry to get home for a fishing trip, went just a shade too fast round one leg of the triangle and failed to get the gear into reverse soon enough, with the result that the stopblock ended up firmly in the hedge, and our cow-catcher was pushed right back onto the front bogie. This was quickly straightened, but not before we had reversed hard into a beautifully-polished Springs 15AR and broken its front coupler. We beat a hasty retreat to the yard before the Shed Foreman could pounce!

One might occasionally be rewarded with a mechanically-fired 15F and although I was

Right: South African Railways narrow (2ft) gauge NG/G16 Class 2-6-2 + 2-6-2 Garratt No E139 pauses during shunting at Donnybrook, Natal on August 11, 1969. *L. A. Nixon*

There are very British-looking signals in the background as SAR GM Class 4-8-2 + 2-8-4 Garratt No 2299 remarshalls its train at Magaliesburg on October 19, 1971. *K. Smith*

happy enough to handle the stoker on shunts or shed duties, I was caught out one day when given a 15F for a round trip working to a place near Pretoria. I shall go into the technicalities of stokers later, but suffice to say here that at this time I hadn't a clue how to handle one on the main line with a heavy load. In a semi-tropical thunderstorm my mate rescued me by firing and driving at his usual breakneck speed simultaneously, while I hung on like grim death trying to make certain through the squalls that we were not passing any signals at danger! It was a thrilling run, undoubtedly my best high-speed trip whilst at Germiston, and I certainly knew how to handle a 15F stoker thereafter! We made up some five hours on the schedule that day, and this meant time credited to us even though we had signed off.

The money on this type of work, and shunts, is good, and with low taxes, and hostel food and accommodation at £15 a month all-in, including a scoff-tin packed for every shift, I found it easy to save, and soon bought a small car — a necessity for getting about and for lineside photography.

My seven months at Germiston taught me to be very wary of native "pranks", and this training was to prove handy at Pietermaritzburg. Near Germiston a goods-only avoiding line runs through a native area. At night it is essential to come to a stand at "reds" in this area with the couplings pulled out tight by advance brake application, and to keep the brakes full on until the signal has cleared, otherwise, natives amuse themselves by pulling the automatic coupler release wires with obvious results! More malicious still was the occasion on which the locking chain of a facing point lever was broken, and the point reversed, with the result that a 15F ran off the main line into a private siding at close on 60mph. The Germiston crew jumped clear in time and survived, but the engine was severely damaged in the resultant pile-up.

After exactly seven months, by which time I was heartily sick of shunting, and the feeling that Germiston was not a proper steam shed in the British tradition, my transfer to Pietermaritzburg came through. A weekend dash ensued, and I arrived in time to see the rows of Garratts dozing on shed at Masons Mill on the Sunday afternoon. Accommodation at the very modern staff hostel was soon arranged, and I was booked out as third man next day on the Franklin run, to familiarise myself with the line and the mechanically-stoked GMA class double 4-8-2s.

Branching south off the electrified Johannesburg-Durban line at Napier Junction, itself just south of Pietermaritzburg, the line to Franklin runs for 140 miles through the most beautiful scenery. Though single throughout, and worked on the staff-and-ticket system, it carries heavy timber and livestock traffic. It twists and turns up moun-

tains and down into valleys without a single tunnel and hardly a mile of straight track throughout. Donnybrook, 83 miles out, is the junction for the lightly-laid Underberg branch, and is also the terminus of the 2ft gauge line from Umzinto on the coast. From Franklin the line splits into two branches, to Kokstad and Matatiele. Both are railheads for the native homelands known as the Transkei, and provide heavy third class passenger traffic.

North from Pietermaritzburg is the 60 mile long goods-only branch to Greytown, running through hilly sugar-cane country and with a ruling gradient of 1 in 27 uncompensated. Four feeder lines branch off this line — at Schroeders to Bruyns Hill (15 miles), at Dalton to Glenside (12 miles), at Chailey to Mount Alida (25 miles) and at Greytown to Kranskop (31 miles). In practice, Masons Mill crews usually only work the line as far as Schroeders (where there is a coal stage), except in the sugar-cane season (May to November), when the line is extremely busy and we worked trains through to the sugar-mill at Jaagbaan on the Glenside branch. Greytown crews work their end of the line, and the branches, the timetable being arranged so that trains from either end of the line met at Schroeders, where loads were exchanged. In practice, however, this did not always work out!

In January 1973, Masons Mill motive power consisted of some 60 or so GMA class double 4-8-2s, 27 GF double Pacifics, and seven lightweight and ageing GCA double 2-6-2s. For light shunts in Pietermaritzburg there are four modern S2 0-8-0s, with several 14R 4-8-2s for Masons Mill and Victoria yards, as well as private siding work. At one time recently the Garratt allocation was over 100, with the influx of a number of GO class double 4-8-2s; but these have now been reallocated to the Durban north coast depot of Empangeni. Most trains on the Franklin and Greytown lines are GMA-hauled, with a high proportion double-headed by two GMAs. On the Greytown line, they usually had auxiliary water tanks coupled between them, and some Franklin line trips were similarly worked, particularly from Masons Mill as far as Donnybrook.

The Underberg branch is worked solely by GCAs which are stationed on the branch and worked down to Masons Mill in rotation on the daily pick-up goods for their fortnightly boiler washouts. The GF double Pacifics handle this working when a GCA is not available, and three or four are also kept at Franklin for the Matatiele branch, also receiving washouts at "the Mill". On the Greytown side GFs work the Bruyns Hill branch and shunt Schroeders, and most trains on the Kranskop and Mount Alida branches from Greytown are GF-hauled. Otherwise, all traffic on this side is GMA-hauled. The branch off the electrified Durban line at Thornville to Richmond is worked by three GFs kept at Richmond but exchanged regularly with freshly washed-out examples from the Mill.

My choice of transfer to Masons Mill soon proved itself. Within a week I was allocated to a Mail Link driver, who with long service had progressed to the "Special Grade" and was probably the best driver there. From the mundane routine of Germiston, I suddenly found myself working mainline passenger trains, with all the responsibilities of keeping to schedules which might seem slow by BR standards, but can tax a fireman's ingenuity to the limit, given the extremely poor Natal coal in use. One might think that life would be easy with mechanical-stoked GMAs on most trains (I would only use the shovel about four or five days a month, with GFs and the occasional 14R on shunts for a bit of relief) but the poor coal, some of it stockpiled for a year and badly affected by long exposure to the sun, is totally unsuited to the requirements of steam engines, and certainly to automatic stokers, which like good quality, evenly-graded coal which is free of slack. Regretably, there is a very large proportion of the latter in the soft Natal coal, and heavy clinkering was unavoidable even if one used the steam-worked grate-rocker every few minutes to keep the fire loose. We regularly cleaned the fire four times per trip to Franklin, and sometimes as often as six, although with passenger trains this would be out of the question and one had to struggle on and hope for the best. As I became more experienced with the two different types of stoker fitted to the GMAs, the work became easier until, during my last few months I had enough confidence to allow my mate to run through booked fire-cleaning places.

A mechanical stoker demands brain rather than brawn and in this respect steam fans have an advantage over firemen who are purely firing to earn a living, and have very little interest in their job. No two GMAs could be fired identically — each had its variations, and one would have to concentrate far more than if hand-firing. The slightest variation in regulator, cut-off, load, gradient, coal quality and steam pressure could throw the even firing of the stoker completely out, leading to huge banks of unburnt coal, clinkering and rapid loss of steam. I found that, above all, the most important factor was knowing your driver and his methods of handling, and vice-versa; in this respect allocation to a regular driver is vital. Once the crew know how each other handles the job, 50 per cent of the work is cut out. I was generally fortunate here, although there were occasions when I found myself booked with another driver due to leave arrangements — fortunately usually only for one isolated turn. On one such occasion I found myself with a young driver well-known as a speed merchant. Regulator well open down the steep banks of the Greytown line was one of his less dangerous tricks, but on this trip he decided to "hit it" uphill also. Now, on the return journey from Schroeders, the last bank from Otto's Bluff to the summit at Claridge is a vicious one, and though only four miles long it has several sharp reverse curves and sections of 1 in 27-30. By this time

the fire is usually well-clinkered and the fireman does not expect the driver to work the engine harder than necessary to keep a steady 10-15mph. We were the leading engine of a double-header, and before I had even had time to fill the boiler and adjust the stoker at Otto's Bluff, my driver had picked up the staff and opened up as if there were a shark on his tail! How we stayed on the rails I shall never know; the fireman of the second engine confided later that he and his mate had been standing at the cab doors ready to jump, with their regulator hardly open. We topped the summit in about six minutes, against the normal allowance of 21, and I must have come as close to dropping a plug at that moment as I shall ever come, yet although my driver was well aware of the non-existent water-level, he clearly hadn't the slightest intention of slowing before we hit the downgrade. This demon of drivers was later reduced to shunting for another speeding incident!

Accidents at Masons Mill were all too frequent. Shortly before I arrived, two firemen and a driver died when a double-header turned over down an embankment, due to excessive speed on the curves. More common, however, were incidents caused by native "pranks". One, more comic than tragic, occurred on my very first day, while travelling as third man to Franklin. We were not far from Franklin, and it was nearly dark, with the GMA pounding steadily upgrade in dry conditions, when we suddenly went into a violent wheelspin on a tight curve in a cutting. With the engine slipping almost to a stand, and sand having no effect, the fireman climbed down, wiped his hands along the rail surface, and returned to show them covered in thick grease! He evidently knew all about this particular trick, because he grabbed a lamp and beckoned to me to follow him down the train. Halfway along, out of sight of both the engine and guards van, several natives were busily unloading a coal truck! They fled on seeing us approach, but I was assured that such

Left: With buck-eye couplers, box-cars and skyscrapers, there is a strong American flavour in this shot of S and S1 Class 0-8-0s at work in Braamfontein yard, Johannesburg in March 1973. *J. D. Mann*

Below: With an additional tank car coupled ahead, a GMAM Class 4-8-2 + 2-8-4 Garratt winds through the outskirts of Pietermaritzburg with a heavy freight for Schroeders on the Greytown branch. Ahead lies a six-mile climb of 9,000ft over gradients as steep as 1 in 30. *J. D. Mann*

Below right: As dawn breaks over Karee Bloemfontein one day in July, 1970, the rising sun silhouettes a 15F Class 4-8-2 rolling by at the head of a freight train. *L. A. Nixon*

incidents were not unusual in that area!

The natives tend to fight among themselves a great deal — and they are none too particular about where they fight. On one occasion the night "mail" to Franklin got only as far as Henley, an hour out of Pietermaritzburg, when fighting broke out on the train. By the time the police arrived, they had seven corpses to deal with! When their pranks involved staff safety, it was different. A ticket Inspector on the Mail one night insisted that we call out the police at Donnybrook — despite the delay this would mean to the entire night passenger traffic — as he had been attacked by a ticketless native who accused his two companions of stealing his money and ticket. When they turned on him, he dived smartly out of the window at a point where we were moving quite fast downgrade. The following train found no trace of him but his two "companions", also ticketless, succumbed to the Inspector who locked them in the lavatory!

More serious was the occasion when a GCA heading the pick-up goods from Masons Mill to Donnybrook ran over a three-foot length of rail wedged upside-down between the running and check rail on a tight curve. Miraculously nothing derailed, though they were doing 30mph. We were returning from Franklin and due to cross them in the next loop beyond the incident. Badly shaken up, they demanded relief and refused to work the train any further. The need for cow-catchers was well demonstrated on the Franklin line — we regularly caught animals of all types, many belonging to natives, who would then retaliate by stoning the crews of trains passing the spot!

Masons Mill had far more atmosphere than Germiston. I enjoyed my time there very much, and could not have wished for a better depot. In seven months there I logged 13,000 miles on "Peacocks" alone (the nickname for Garratts). One has to be prepared to work hard, with little spare time — rest days are unheard of — but it is well worth the experience, and there are always vacancies for firemen, though this steam stronghold was to receive its first allocation of diesels in 1974.

Rails Across Rannoch

Below: Stanier Class 5 4-6-0s Nos 45213 and 45487 restart the 12·05 Oban-Glasgow away from Tyndrum Lower and head for the West Highland main line at Crianlarich on April 3 1961. *G. T. Robinson*

Right: Standard Class 5 4-6-0 No 73078 pilots Stanier Class 5 4-6-0 No 44975 out of Fort William with the 13·00 Mallaig-Glasgow (Queen Street) on May 26 1961. During 1975, a new station was built at Fort William on a site beside the track just behind the camera, and the section of line seen here, together with the old station, has become the site of a new road. *M. Mensing*

Bottom right: Holmes ex-North British Railway J36 Class 0-6-0 No 65313 indulges in some leisurely shunting outside Fort William in early British Railways days. *Eric Treacy*

Above: Complete with high-sided weatherproof tender, Fowler Class 4F 0-6-0 No 44255 saunters into Roy Bridge station with a lightweight permanent way train on May 24 1961. *M. Mensing*

Below: Raindrops from an early morning April shower still hang on the railings as BR Standard Class 5 4-6-0 No 73078 comes to a stand in Fort William Station with the 5·45 from Glasgow. *G. F. Heiron*

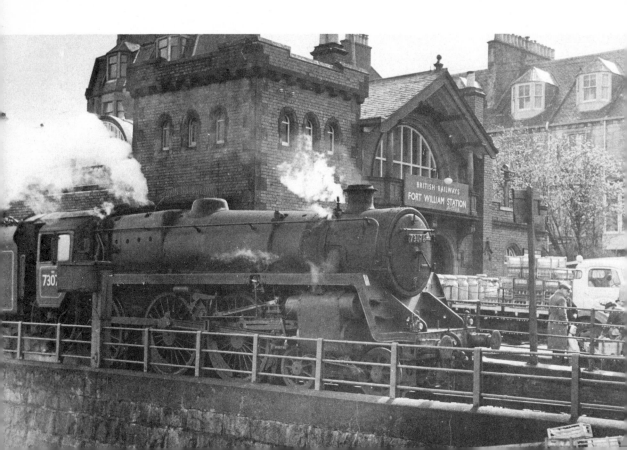

Above: Cantering up to Mallaig Junction, on the outskirts of Fort William, comes K1 Class 2-6-0 No 62012 with a lengthy freight for the Mallaig line on May 22 1961. *M. Mensing*

Below: It is a little before noon on June 11 1951 and Class K2/2 2-6-0 No 61774 *Loch Garry* is easing the 8.45 special express fish train from Mallaig past Mallaig Junction signalbox and onto the main line, so that sister engine No 61764 *Loch Arkaig* waiting in the background can back down and take the train on to Glasgow without delay. *E. D. Bruton*

Top left: Pulling smartly away from the now-closed
station at Shandon is push-pull fitted North British Class
C15 4-4-2T No 67460 with the 13·05 Arrochar &
Tarbet-Craigendoran on a fine June day in 1958.
W. J. V. Anderson

Left: Curving across one of the many bridges that span
the upland bogs of Rannoch Moor, BR Standard Class 5
4-6-0 No 73078 and Class K2/2 2-6-0 No 61787 *Loch
Quoich* head for lonely Rannoch station with a heavy
Glasgow-Fort William train on May 26 1959.
S. E. Teasdale

Right: Having completed its shunting duties at the
Aluminium plant and Mallaig Junction, ex-North British
J36 Class 0-6-0 No 65300 heads for Fort William with a
short train of alumina wagons on May 22 1961.
M. Mensing

Below: With their vigorous exhausts adding to the drama
of the scene, a pair of Class 5s, one BR Standard, the
other Stanier, storm up through the rugged Monessie
Gorge alongside the Spean towards Rannoch with an
afternoon Mallaig-Glasgow express in March 1961
G. F. Heiron

Left: The much-photographed BR Standard Class 5 4-6-0 No 73078 seems to have spent most of its life on the West Highland line on pilot duties! But here at least it is doing the lion's share of the work as it leads an unidentified B1 Class 4-6-0 beneath the bridge on the approach to Tulloch station with the 15·10 Fort William-Glasgow train on a perfect Highland day in August 1961. *S. C. Crook*

Below: With the hills beyond providing a dramatic Highland backcloth, one of Fort William's own K2/2 Class 2-6-0s, No 61788 *Loch Rannoch* marshals a freight outside its home depot. *Eric Treacy*

Top right: With safety valves beginning to lift despite the 1 in 60 climb from Crianlarich, Eastfield B1 Class 4-6-0 No 61243 *Sir Harold Mitchell* breasts County March summit, on the borders of Argyll and Perthshire, with a Glasgow-Fort William freight on May 7 1956. *J. B. Welldon*

Right: North British Locomotive Co Type 2 Diesel-electric No D6137 pilots preserved North British Class D34 4-4-0 No 256 *Glen Douglas* down into picturesque Tulloch station with a special bound for Fort William on June 1 1963 after the rostered pilot, a J37 Class 0-6-0, had failed at Rannoch. *G. W. Morrison*

Scenes from Waterloo

Southern Railway engines were used to sharing their tracks with electric trains long before it became a familiar practice elsewhere, but nowhere was this more evident than at Waterloo, where steam and electric traction co-existed for over 50 years. Top right is a view of the station on a Saturday morning in March 1932 with D15 Class 4-4-0 No E471 ready to depart with the 12·40 West of England express — this was a Salisbury King Arthur turn on other days of the week — and an Ashford-built U Class Mogul at the head of the 12·50 to Portsmouth. This was just before the section prefix letters were eliminated from the original numbers in favour of renumbering in the 1000 and 2000 series for SECR and LBSCR engines respectively. Top far right is much the same view of the station about two years later, this time in the late afternoon. Passengers on the left bid their last farewells as Urie King Arthur Class 4-6-0 No 751 *Etarre* prepares to depart with the 16·50 express to Portsmouth while on the right sister Maunsell "Scotch" Arthur No 777 *Sir Lamiel* simmers quietly at the head of the 17·00 West of England express. The prefix letters have now disappeared and smoke deflectors are becoming a common sight on all the larger classes of engine.

Just over three decades later, in 1967, the Maunsell electric stock which pushed the Arthurs off the Portsmouth Direct line in 1937 was soon to be replaced itself. Still in green, but now with BR-type 'raspberry' horns and an early form of yellow warning panel (bottom right) 2-BIL No 2039 waits to depart for Wimbledon Park Sidings on July 2, whilst alongside BRCW Type 3 No D6543 is ready with the 13·30 Weymouth train.

Only inches away from the long hydraulic buffers and cheek-by-jowl with one of the ubiquitous 4-SUB suburban electric units stands rebuilt West Country Class Pacific No 34100 *Appledore* (bottom far right) after arrival with an up evening train from Bournemouth in December 1965. *G. J. Jefferson (2), R. Warren, G. F. Heiron*

G.E. Byways In Norfolk

R. Powell Hendry

Few areas of Britain are more distinctive than Norfolk, with the broads and its quaint pebble wall buildings — on anything from barns to churches. The county has much to attract the ordinary holidaymaker and had much of interest to the railway enthusiast, for this was the only area in which the Great Eastern Railway met any serious competition, except on its borders. Throughout the whole of North Norfolk stretched the tentacles of the Midland & Great Northern Joint Railway — 'Marriott's Tramway', as it was derisively called. Lowestoft, Yarmouth, Walsham, Cromer, Norwich, Aylsham, Fakenham, Lynn — wherever one turned the tiny M&GN challenged the Liverpool Street empire. As a result both the GE and the Joint probably tried that little bit harder. Would, for instance, the GE have lavished such care on their Norwich-Lynn service had the Joint line via Melton not existed? Especially as the trains which used the south curve at Dereham completely missed the station — the most important on the line!

This article recalls briefly the various GE lines centred on Dereham, Swaffham, Kings Lynn and Wells. Perhaps the best known of these lines was the Hunstanton branch, familiar to countless holidaymakers over the years, and for the many journeys made by the Royal family to Wolferton for nearby Sandringham. The line was 15¼ miles long, double as far as Wolferton, and possessed five intermediate stations. Beyond Wolferton (6¼ miles) it was worked on the electric tablet system. Wolferton — 'the' royal station — was until recent years a joy to behold, and had the station remained open, an extension to the waiting room to house the ever-growing collection of best kept station certificates would have been essential!

The last station before Hunstanton was Heacham, junction for the West Norfolk branch to Wells. The junction with the West Norfolk line faced up the line towards Lynn, but ironically most trains in GE days reversed here and ran into Hunstanton! A 39ft 8in turntable was installed at Heacham — one of the smallest in the area, for those at Hunstanton and Wells were 49ft 9in and 44ft 8in respectively.

The Hunstanton line service was, as one would expect, highly seasonal in nature, but in latter GE days a basic winter service of nine or ten trains each way was provided, with some through workings to Liverpool Street, Cambridge or Ely. In the winter of 1919, the first departure, the 7.02am, included a restaurant car and was due into platform 10 at Liverpool Street at 10.23am. The return working arrived back in Hunstanton at 9.13pm. A common latterday GE practice was the attaching of fitted wagons to selected trains to convey urgent cattle, horse, or perishable traffic off the overnight London goods. On the Hunstanton line, the 10.15am ex-Lynn was allowed to take wagons off the London goods forward to Hunstanton. In the return direction, train No 13, the 1.45pm was authorised to convey 'road trucks' to pick up urgent goods from intermediate stations.

The 18¼ mile West Norfolk branch was rather longer than the main Hunstanton line and was worked on the staff system, the only intermediate block post being at Docking. To the historically minded the line had several interesting associations; at Burnham Market the traveller was but a short distance from the birthplace of Admiral Lord Nelson, and at

Holkham, the next station, one might see produce being loaded from Holkham Hall, home of the great 18th century agricultural reformer Coke. The West Norfolk enjoyed a less frequent service than the Hunstanton line; in 1919 four trains ran each way between Wells and Heacham, three of them then reversing for the short run into Hunstanton. The fourth gave up the ghost and hung around Heacham for a while and then, as with the other three, returned whence it came. On Saturdays an extra service from Wells was provided; this originated from Norwich and ran via Dereham to Wells, reversed at Wells, then ran via Heacham to Lynn! A daily goods ran out from Lynn over the branch and was due in Wells at 2.35pm. Usually the goods started its return trip at 4.05pm, but on Tuesdays it left at 3.12pm in order to clear the line for the Tuesdays Only cattle special from Lynn to Wells, which it crossed at Heacham. The engine and van off the special worked home later in the evening. When required, a trip working was provided between Hunstanton and Docking, taking just under three hours. The first down train, the 8.35am from Heacham, was permitted to convey two cattle wagons from Docking or Burnham Market to Wells, but "the Docking and Burnham Market Station Masters to arrange that cattle is only accepted at one station for this train on any one day". One can imagine the reaction of a Docking farmer on being told — "Sorry, you can't send cattle out on the 8.51 — its Burnham's turn to-day"!

The steeply graded approach to Wells gave rise to quite severe operating problems, and when goods trains were too long to be run round in Wells yard, the dividing and dropping of wagons down into the station had to be supervised by the Foreman Porter who, knowing his station, could be expected to be cautious. He was in fact a highly versatile personage, for in addition to dropping down wagons he doubled up in his spare time as a sort of 'banking staff', being required to travel on the footplate of any engine banking a

heavy West Norfolk passenger train out of the station as far as the down home signal!

After passenger services ceased, working goods trains over the Heacham-Burnham section became a protracted business for the line was treated as a 'light railway' and, in addition to two ungated crossings, there were five at which the gates were opened by train crews and only one, at Docking, where station staff were on hand to open the gates. The key which unlocked the gates was kept with the single line staff in Heacham cabin and had to be collected (along with the staff!) before a train worked out onto the branch.

Wells in its heyday must have been a fascinating station, and had an allocation of at least four engines to work the Norwich and Lynn lines. In the winter of 1919 there were in addition to the four West Norfolk trains, seven passenger trains each way to Norwich during the day. On Saturdays, two extra trains arrived at Wells; one, as already mentioned, then departed to Lynn, while the other returned as empty stock to Dereham at 6.05pm. A twice-daily freight worked by Wells and Norwich engines operated north of Dereham; over the last $4\frac{1}{2}$ miles from Walsingham into Wells goods trains were limited to 20 wagons on arriving trains and 25 for departures. Although Walsingham was a block post, trains were not permitted to cross here (!) and the first crossing point was Fakenham (latterly Fakenham East), the present railhead. Fakenham was an interesting station, for it was built early on in the railway age, and the rectangular, almost Georgian, buildings were nearly at rail level. In later years when the platform was raised steps down into the rooms were provided!

South of Fakenham the line crossed a number of minor roads on the level; one of these minor crossings, near Ryburgh, was rather unusual, for in addition to the crossing keeper's cottage (which on account of the largish family of one incumbent had been extended by using a rather venerable carriage as a bedroom/annexe!) there was on the op-

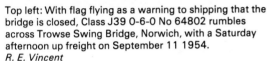

Top left: With flag flying as a warning to shipping that the bridge is closed, Class J39 0-6-0 No 64802 rumbles across Trowse Swing Bridge, Norwich, with a Saturday afternoon up freight on September 11 1954.
R. E. Vincent

Left: Known locally as the "Crab and Winkle", the Thetford-Swaffham line was one of the haunts of Holden's GER Class E4 2-4-0s. Here No 62793, one of the class fitted with side-window cabs, fusses along near Watton on October 13 1951.   *G. J. Jefferson*

Centre top: September 7 1968 was the last day of service on the Dereham-Kings Lynn section, and this Metro-Cammell twin unit is apparently more than sufficient for the traffic on offer as it calls at Middleton Towers, last stop before Kings Lynn, on the 14·34 from Dereham. The white dusting on the track is not early Autumn snow, but spillage of sand from wagons working off the quarry branch just visible in the background — a traffic which has kept the section of line from here on to Kings Lynn open.   *John Vaughan*

Top right: Dropping down from the junction at Trowse under the Norwich-Ipswich main line at Hartford Bridges comes K3 Class 2-6-0 No 61867 with the 11·33 Yarmouth Vauxhall-Sheffield Victoria on a Summer Saturday in the mid-50s.   *R. E. Vincent*

Below: The line northwards from Kings Lynn to Heacham and Hunstanton, and at one time Wells, was of special interest because it served Wolferton, station for Sandringham and starting point for Royal holidays for many decades. But the Beeching axe was no respecter of tradition; first the line was singled and then, in 1969, closed completely. During the final week of operation, a Metro-Cammell twin unit slows into Snettisham past the already disused signalbox on the 14·04 Hunstanton-Kings Lynn working on April 29 1969.   *G. R. Mortimer*

posite side of the road a small hut for use when the crossing keeper was ill or on holiday and a replacement was called for!

Just 15½ miles south of Wells was the curiously named County School, junction for the Wroxham line. On the Wells-Dereham section Fakenham and County School were the main crossing places, and although North Elmham possessed a loop, passenger trains were not permitted to cross there, so its use was limited. North of this point the ordinary train staff sufficed but for the short distance on to Dereham electric tablet instruments were installed.

Dereham, or more correctly East Dereham, seemed to be more railway dominated than even Melton Constable, for although there was no railway works, the station, the various junctions and yards, and the innumerable level crossings made it appear that the railway quite engulfed the town. Dereham station was sited at the north end of the triangle close by the main road crossing, which was controlled by the North Cabin. Dereham Station box,

264 yards to the South, controlled the junction with the north curve onto the Swaffham line, while a further 364 yards brought one to Dereham South Junction box, beyond which lay a couple more level crossings within 100 yards of each other.

One of the main reasons for the retention of this section of line for freight is the quite busy traffic to and from Fison's fertilizer works at Dereham. Nowadays large bogie wagons handle the traffic, but throughout the siding's history care has been called for in shunting. The LNER regulations for working traffic were quite amusing: "when traffic is being loaded or unloaded from wagons at these sidings, a red flag by day and a red light during darkness is to be exhibited by Fison's peo-

Storming out of Kings Lynn station and past the shed comes D16/3 Class 4-4-0 No 62601 with the Hunstanton portion of an express on August 19 1952. On the right, J17 Class 0-6-0 No 65568, complete with BR-fitted tender cab, waits its turn to proceed with a freight train. *P. J. Lynch*

ple from the second story of the malting"! Similar regulations applied to Gray's Granary by the West Junction, for it was feared that their lorries might foul one of the sidings.

Between Dereham and Wymondham, the junction with the Thetford-Norwich main line, there were four more stations. Perhaps the most interesting operating practice on this section concerned Thuxton, for at this station the yard was controlled from a ground frame and the key was kept in the box at Hardingham, the next station to the south. When a down train required to shunt Thuxton, the guard collected the key from the Hardingham signalman and in due course handed it over at Yaxham, the next station beyond Thuxton, where the person in charge was required to return the key 'by the first means'!

In GE days about eight passenger trains were provided each way between Dereham and Norwich, and connections were made at Dereham for the Wroxham line and Wells or Lynn as the case might be. Passengers awaiting connections were well catered for, however, for the station boasted its own refreshment room!

The 23½ mile County School-Wroxham branch diverged from the Wells line six miles north of Dereham. A little over 15 miles of this line remains in use to-day for freight, from Wroxham to near Reepham, where a new connection has been laid in to the ex-M&GN Norwich line, which has been cut back to Lenwade. Nowadays the branch is served out of Wensum yard, Norwich but in the early 1920s six passenger trains worked over the line each way from Dereham to Norwich, plus a daily goods service. The most important station on the section was Aylsham (latterly Aylsham South) which even into the 1970s retained much of its bygone atmosphere. Unlike Cawston and Reepham, which possessed that peculiarly GE idea, the block telegraph hut and outside ground frame, Aylsham had a small but picturesque signal cabin.

The third line from Dereham was the Lynn line, of which only the Lynn-Middleton section and the stub of the North curve to the West Junction level crossing now remain. For many years the most important station on this section was Swaffham, junction for the line down to Roudham Junction and Thetford. Swaffham was a fairly large station, with an extensive yard and goods warehouse, and boasted (as did Dereham) a 45ft 0in turntable. It was not only a physical junction but a district boundary; west of Swaffham, and west of Wells on the West Norfolk branch, for accident and emergency purposes the lines came under the control of Kings Lynn. To the east, however, the Wells-Wymondham, County School-Wroxham, Swaffham-Dereham and Swaffham-Roudham lines all came under Norwich Thorpe which, with its 35 ton steam crane, had the second largest crane on the whole GE section in 1947.

On the Lynn-Dereham section the GE provided seven or eight passenger workings a day, and a twice-daily goods. As was usual in the area, the service was somewhat altered on Tuesdays and an additional Cattle Special was run from Lynn to cope with livestock traffic.

Some of the Thetford branch trains made quite good connections with the Lynn-Dereham services at Swaffham but a few for inexplicable reasons adopted the modern practice of 'just missing' the connection! The single line Thetford branch diverged at the east end of Swaffham station and ran for 18½ miles to Roudham Junction, where it joined the main Norwich-Ely line, facing towards the latter. The five or so passenger trains which used the branch each day ran on the short distance into Thetford, but the single out and back goods working each day from Lynn terminated at Roudham. As usual, cattle working was of considerable importance, and all intermediate stations were required to advise Roudham by 2.45pm when they had cattle to load. In the 1920s 'cattles' were quite a common sight in the yards, and horse boxes appeared from time to time. On one occasion one of the 'school trains' (for Thetford Grammar School) picked up nine boxes at Watton and four more at Wretham and Hockham — quite an increase on its usual load of three six-wheelers!

In the early twenties the morning and evening school trains were worked by two venerable GE 'bogies', but as an improvement these were replaced about the time of the Grouping by the three six-wheelers, one of which carried the boys, one the girls and one, presumably, the rest!

The run from Watton into Thetford was always enjoyable, with miles and miles of heather and, in season, countless Marguerites brightening up the scene. At Thetford, passengers were rarely allowed to forget where they were, for the foreman porter's voice bellowing "Thetford — change here for Swaffham and Bury lines" could be heard the length of the station!

On the 26½ mile Dereham-Lynn line the main crossing points were Wendling, Dunham, Swaffham, Narborough and East Winch. Nowadays the only part of the line to carry train services is the 3¼ mile section out from Lynn to Middleton — now Middleton Towers — to serve what is now 'British Industrial Sand, Middleton' but what in GE days was Boam's Sidings. In 1919 Boam's were served by a trip working out of Lynn at 1.00pm. An engine and van worked out to East Winch where they ran round, picked up any GE or Boam empty wagons left by the 4.44pm from Dereham the previous day, and then ran back to Middleton where there was almost an hour for shunting before returning to Lynn at 2.28pm. Another working which served Boam's sidings when required was the 3.35pm goods back from Roudham Junction on the Thetford-Swaffham line.

At Kings Lynn the GER provided extensive facilities, for in addition to the main passenger station and yard, there was (and still is) a very busy level crossing, which until the building of the Lynn bypass was the main cause of long traffic jams at summer weekends. There was also the triple junction to Hunstanton, Dereham and Ely, the Harbour branch, the Docks branch and the M&GN connection.

The working of the Harbour and Dock branches was most interesting. In the early 1920s, three GE and two or three Joint Line trips were made over the Harbour line daily and it was worked on the 'one engine in steam' principle, with a green wooden staff for the single line section from Kings Lynn Harbour Junction box (which also controlled the connection to the M&GN line) to the Wisbech level crossing. In 1919 one engine was in steam daily to work the Harbour branch from 5.30am to about 7.45pm.

In Lynn Town yard, two engines were available for general shunting work, with an additional two engines in steam on Tuesdays to handle the cattle traffic. On the Docks branch, which began in Lynn yard, traffic was worked on an 'as required' basis from 7.00am. The single line section — which was denoted by Engine stop boards — was worked on the train staff system, but without tickets, and the staff itself was normally kept in the yard hut. When the first train was ready to go out onto the Dock branch, the shunter in charge collected the staff and rode with the engine crew on the footplate. The driver kept the staff with his engine until he returned to the yard, or until a second engine and train was ready to proceed onto the branch, in which case the shunter in charge had to collect the staff and walk back to Lynn yard where he would join the crew on the engine of the second train and conduct it onto the branch. If, as sometimes happened, a third engine was required in the Docks, he had to go through the same ritual yet again. Why one wonders was not normal staff and ticket working introduced? It would certainly have been much simpler than 'staff and shunter in charge' working, but would have required accurate information as to how many trains were to follow during the day before the first train set out, and as the line was only worked 'as required', this would not always have been possible to ascertain first thing in the morning.

Apart from the peculiarities of staff working, the Docks branch was hard on shunters in other respects, for so sharp were some of the curves that one man had to preceed the engine by some 30yards and make his hand signals to a colleague, who in turn repeated them to the Engineman! In poor visibility, working the Docks branch became a real headache and Lynn yard would be virtually without shunters at such a time for as many additional men as were necessary were used to maintain communications. One cannot help but feel that a chain of perhaps four or five shunters was not the best way to relay a message quickly and accurately!

In British Railways days Lynn retained many of its peculiarities, not the least of which was a passenger train, the down Night Mail, which was booked to stop at the Junction box to pick up the yard inspector who then accompanied the train into No. 3 platform. This curious method of working was due to the fact that Kings Lynn yard box was closed at night, and although the inspector was allowed to go up into the cabin to restore the signals to their normal position after the arrival of the mail, he was thereafter not allowed to work the box in the normal way.

Instead, he would accompany the mail 'wrong line' back over the Down Main as far as the junction box, where the engine would run round the train, propell the carriages back into No. 3 platform again and then run to shed via the junction box, all the while, of course, ignoring the yard box signals, now all at danger, upon the authority of the Inspector who rode on the footplate! Had these antics been performed in daylight they would have made a fascinating subject for a cine film, but in many ways they were typical of train operation in Norfolk.

In an article of this sort one can no more than touch on the subject, but the object has been to cast a little light on what, in their heyday 50 years ago, must have been a fascinating group of lines.

The only part of the former Midland and Great Nortnern Joint system still to carry passengers by 1970 was the short section from Cromer on to Sheringham, including the one time expansive M&GN terminus at Cromer Beach. On August 29 1970, having come off this last outpost of the M&GN back on to the GE, two Metro-Cammell twin units draw into the tiny but neat Salhouse station on the 10·25 Sheringham-Norwich working.
G. R. Mortimer

Bridges — Rebuilt, Rejuvenated and Rejected

Chris Heaps

During the evening of 21 December 1973 the German motor vessel *Ostediek* collided with the supports of the Swing Bridge at Goole on the ex-North Eastern Railway line between Doncaster and Hull and one of the fixed spans, weighing some 260 tons, crashed down into the River Ouse. Less than eight months later, on 5 August 1974, it was possible to introduce a restricted service using only one of the tracks over the bridge, and by 7 October, less than ten months after the accident, both tracks had been reinstated and normal service resumed.

Just over 13 years previously, on 25 October 1960, a similar disaster befell one of the longest bridges in the British Isles, the Severn Bridge on the ex-GW and Midland Severn and Wye Joint Railway. In thick fog and at night, two tank barges carrying petroleum collided with one of the piers of this 4,161ft long bridge, the collision and subsequent explosion causing one pier and two of the 22 spans to collapse into the River Severn over 70ft below. Although at the time of the disaster the track on the line was being improved and the bridge strengthened to take heavier trains so as to serve as an alternative route for the heavy goods traffic then routed through the Severn Tunnel, the bridge was never

Chastened by the Tay Bridge Disaster, the North British Railway took no chances with the design for their bridge across the other great water barrier to their East Coast Route, the Forth. By any standards, the Forth Bridge is huge, both in overall dimensions and in the size of the individual girders, which here quite dwarf Class 26 No 5302 and Class 47 No 1972 as they double-head an Aberdeen-Edinburgh train off the southern most of the three cantilever spans on April 20 1972. *David Cross*

rebuilt and has now been completely dismantled.

The differing outcomes of these two disasters can, no doubt, be explained by the relative importance of the lines using the damaged bridges — the former is a main link between towns of some size and part of an Inter-City route, whereas the latter was merely a single-track branch with more diversionary potential than day to day importance. Certainly, too, the cost of rebuilding the Severn Bridge would greatly have exceeded the expense incurred at Goole (the reconstruction is estimated to have cost £300,000) as the Goole bridge was short and low when compared to the lofty girders that spanned the wide and deep Severn Estuary.

The two examples do show, however, how a major engineering work can prove the weak, and if damaged possibly fatal, link in a railway whose present or potential importance, whether economically or socially, cannot justify major expenditure.

Probably the most famous example of the rebuilding of a major bridge is that of the present structure across the Tay. Plans for bridging the wide estuary of the River Tay loomed large in the dreams of the shareholders and directors of the North British Railway during the mid-19th Centry, but it was not until 1870 that an Act of Parliament was obtained authorising its construction. By the time the Act received the Royal Assent on 15 July 1870, however, plans were already well advanced for its construction to the designs of Thomas Bouch, and the foundation stone was laid less than a year later, in May 1871. Troubles began to beset the bridge in 1873, when the contractor, Charles de Bergue, died. Then, soon after, it was discovered that the rock bed in mid-river, upon which the plans had been formulated, did not, in fact, exist. Bouch had to make substantial amendments to the design, including lengthening the central and higher spans from 200ft to 245ft, but nevertheless by 1877 this major engineering work had been completed.

The two mile long bridge was ceremonially opened on 31 May 1878 and only three weeks later Queen Victoria inspected the masterpiece from the comfort of the Royal Train on her way from Balmoral to Windsor. On 26 June, at Windsor, Bouch received the honour of a Knighthood in recognition of his great work.

But as it is now well known, less than 18 months later, during a sudden and violent storm on the evening of 28 December 1879, the Tay Bridge was destroyed, and with it the reputation of Sir Thomas. At 5.27pm on that fateful day North British Railway 4-4-0 No. 224 set out from Burntisland with its train for Dundee; shortly before 7pm the train set out across the bridge and seconds later crashed to its destruction in the stormy waters of the Tay Estuary with the loss of all passengers and crew when the 13 "High Girders" collapsed as the train was passing through. Bouch was already preparing designs for an even greater bridge across the Firth of Forth, but his plans were shelved after his dramatic fall from grace.

Notwithstanding the enormity of the disaster, the expense of a new bridge so soon and the engineering problems to be overcome, the North British Railway had established the importance of a rail link across the Tay Estuary both to the peoples of the area, especially Dundee, and to its own shareholders, during the brief period of operation between mid 1878 and 1879. There was therefore no real opposition to proposals for a new bridge, provided that its strength and stability could be assured. By July 1881, the New Tay Viaduct Act had been passed, and soon a double track replacement bridge (Bouch's had been single track) was under construction 60ft upstream from the old, this time to the design of W. H. Barlow, who had been a member of the Court of Enquiry into the disaster, and his son, C. Barlow. Ironically, some of Bouch's old wrought iron girders were re-used in the new structure, although of course entirely new "High Girders" were provided, the new

When an errant tanker brought down two spans of the Severn Bridge on a foggy night in October 1960, the Western Region was in the midst of strengthening the structure so that it could take heavier locomotives and thus provide a useful alternative route to South Wales when the Severn Tunnel was either congested or closed for maintenance. After protracted consideration, the Western Region, probably rightly, decided that the cost of replacing two spans and a pier, and repairing the others, was simply not justified merely to provide an alternative route, and shortly after this shot (Above) of the damaged bridge and its overgrown approach tracks was taken, demolition work began, four years after the accident. The GW 2-8-0 about to pass under the approach viaduct is heading north with a freight on the Severn Tunnel Junction-Gloucester line. Whereas the Severn Bridge collapsed because of a violent impact which no designer could have foreseen, the first Tay Bridge simply blew down, complete with passing train, in a severe but not extraordinary gale 80 years earlier, on December 28 1879, (Below). The subsequent Inquiry discovered that, for a number of reasons, Thomas Bouch's bridge was not as strong as he had supposed, so the remainder was dismantled and a new, double track structure was erected alongside (top right); in this view from Wormit, with Dundee ranged in the background along the far shore, preserved A4 Class Pacific No 4498 *Sir Nigel Gresley* is approaching with a southbound special on May 20 1967. The Menai Bridge, on the other hand, was effectively destroyed from within by a deliberately started fire, and although when the flames were finally quenched the structure remained standing, the tubular girders were badly distorted, visibly sagging between the smoke-blackened piers (centre right). Unlike the Severn Bridge, the bridge across the Menai Straits was a vital link between the mainland and the important ferry and container terminal at Holyhead on the Isle of Anglesey, so British Rail rebuilt the bridge as a single track structure on more modern lines but using the original piers (bottom). *B. J. Ashworth, British Rail, J. R. P. Hunt, J. H. Bird*

bridge being opened to traffic on 20 June 1887. So successful was the new design that the first major overhaul was not necessary until 1965 and it remains in use today, very much as it was built, carrying heavy diesel-hauled East Coast main line express traffic, as well as freight.

The only modern equivalent of the Tay Bridge disaster and subsequent rebuilding (although happily, without loss of life) is the story of the Britannia Tubular Bridge in North Wales. This originally double track link across the Menai Strait was designed for the Chester and Holyhead Railway by Robert Stephenson and followed in concept his design for the Conway Bridge. But whereas the Conway Bridge was only 18ft above water level, Admiralty Regulations of the time required that the proposed railway bridge across the Straits between Caernarvonshire and Anglesey should allow adequate clearance for sailing ships, and the bridge had to be over 120ft above high water level. The bridge took the form of two continuous wrought iron box-section tubes, supported by hefty towers. The tubes were fabricated in sections on shore and floated out into position and, when all were in position, they were united to form a pair of continuous box-section beams 1,511ft long with the tracks running through them. The final rivet was ceremonially closed by Stephenson in March 1850, and the bridge remained in daily use, bearing ever increasing loads, until disaster struck in May 1970.

After the bridge had been completed, the two wrought iron tubes were protected by a timber roof, and early in the present century this roof was renewed using steel trusses and timber boarding sealed with tarred hessian. Further applications of tar were made from time to time thereafter, to keep the surface weatherproof. Notwithstanding the passage of steam trains through the tubes for over a century, there is little evidence that fire was considered a major hazard, although in June 1946, the Down "Irish Mail" was reported to

have passed "a wall of flame" when crossing the bridge. This fire is believed to have been caused by the careless use of a painter's blow lamp, but the tubes were not seriously damaged and the line was re-opened after four days.

How lucky the LMS had been at that time did not become completely obvious until 1970, when the fire alarm was raised at 7.40pm on Saturday, 23 May. Two young boys, using burning newspapers as torches, went into the tubes in search of bats and birds nests, and accidentally set fire to the bridge. The fire quickly spread to the timber roof and the flames, fanned by a strong wind, raged out of control for over nine hours. At the height of the fire, the iron tubes became white hot, cooling and contracting again as the fire burnt itself out. Subsequent inspection showed that as a result of this ordeal by fire, the tubes had split from top to bottom at each tower along the original construction joints, and that the main tubes had sagged by no less than 29in at the centre of their span. It was clear that the tubes were in a highly unstable condition and that therefore the line could not be re-opened for some time, thus effectively cutting all rail access to the Isle of Anglesey.

As in the case of the Tay Bridge, the importance of rail traffic over the bridge, in particular to the Container Terminal at Holyhead and a nuclear power station in the north of the island, necessitated the restoration of the rail link as soon as possible. Although the restoration has taken place within the impressive original towers of the bridge, designed for Stephenson by the architect, Francis Thompson, the reconstruction of the bridge has been of such major proportions and to such an entirely new concept, that it would be true to say that a new bridge has been constructed.

No longer do Admiralty requirements demand generous clearances above high water level, and the tubular concept dictated by such requirements in the 19th Century has been abandoned. Two arched steel latticed structures with a clearance of only 90ft above

the Strait have been constructed at a cost of over £3million, and provision has been made for the addition of a three-lane road deck above the railway track at a later date if required. The bridge has been rebuilt as a single track structure and was brought back into operation, although not all works had been completed, on the night of 30/31 January 1972, less than two years after the fire.

A bridge that has completely succumbed to that enemy of the railway, the motor car, is that at Connel Ferry on the ex-Callender and Oban Railway Ballachulish Branch in Scotland. Opened in 1903 across the end of Loch Etive, fast currents made it impracticable to construct piers for a normal bridge and necessitated the use of the cantilever principle, the practicality of which had been amply demonstrated in the construction of the Forth Bridge in 1890. The Connel Ferry bridge's centre span of 524ft, although some way behind, is still second only in length in the British Isles to the clear spans of 1,710ft on the Forth Bridge. From the outset the Bridge carried not only the single track Ballachulish branch but also a single track road, movement over which was controlled by the railway signalman. The Railway Company had priority, as befitted the builders and owners of the bridge, but the motor car has had its revenge and has ruled absolutely since the closure of the branch in 1966, one of the con-

ditions of which was that the bridge should be maintained and given over entirely to road use.

The Connel Ferry Bridge was designed by Sir John Wolfe Barry, but in collaboration with his two partners, E. Cruttwell and H. M. Brunel. This Brunel was the son of Isambard Kingdom Brunel who, it may be recalled, in addition to planning and executing hundreds of miles of main railway line, designing locomotives and building ships, also managed to find time to design one or two major bridges. The Clifton Suspension Bridge over the Avon Gorge at Bristol was a road bridge constructed to Brunel's design after his death, but his railway bridges at Chepstow and Saltash are rightly famous as major examples of his railway engineering work.

The design of Chepstow Bridge, across the River Wye, was, like the Britannia bridge at Menai, determined by navigational requirements and, like the Britannia Bridge, it has since been so rebuilt that little of the original design remains. The original Bridge, opened in 1852, was based on the suspension principle later used at Saltash, and gave a 50ft headroom above high water level. In 1962 extensive corrosion of the track and cross girders was discovered and because navigational requirements are no longer of importance, it was decided to replace the suspension spans with modern steel trusses of unexceptional design.

In contrast, the Royal Albert Bridge at Saltash, on the county boundary between Devon and Cornwall, has seen little change since it was built to Brunel's design for the Cornwall Railway in 1859, although strengthening work was carried out by BR in 1967 and 1968 to permit the use of heavier trains. In the design of this Bridge, Brunel once again faced problems similar to those solved by Stephenson at Menai — the insistence by the Admiralty on large spans and ample head room. But, Brunel faced an additional problem in that there was no sound island in the middle of the River Tamar similar to the Britannia Rock upon which the centre pier of the brige could be built. He solved the problem by constructing a central pier in the middle of the channel and resting on it from each side two 455ft spans formed of huge, arched wrought iron oval tubes. Suspended from each side of each tube are the giant suspension chains, and these in turn support the deck. In his design, Brunel developed his theories and experience gained during the design and construction of the smaller and lower Chepstow Bridge, and since the latter has now been rebuilt, Saltash remains as the only major railway bridge in use in the United Kingdom to-day constructed on the suspension principle. The Bridge was opened by Prince Albert on 2 May 1859, but tests over a century later in 1967 showed that only minor modifications were necessary to strengthen the bridge to withstand the stresses of modern traffic. When one considers the difference in weight between the trains of to-day and the lightweight, short trains generally in use when such structures were designed, the fact that only minor modifications were re-

quired to the original design after such a period speaks volumes for the skill of men such as Brunel and of the Contractors by whom such bridges were painstakingly erected.

Save for the Severn Bridge, the fate of which was sealed by an accident, the other bridges mentioned so far remain in use, albeit, in some cases, in a rather different form from the original designs. Other major engineering works have, regrettably, already been demolished, the lines they served having fallen into disuse. Notable among these were the graceful Crumlin Viaduct in South Wales and the spidery but efficient viaducts designed by the unfortunate Sir Thomas Bouch in Westmorland and County Durham.

The Belah and Deepdale Viaducts, on the South Durham and Lancashire Union Line to Tebay and Penrith, were specifically designed to be built from a range of standardised components and were erected in the rugged Pennine country in 1859, some years before Bouch's peak of fame and subsequent disgrace. Outwardly flimsy-looking in construction, both nevertheless survived until the line was closed just over a century later in 1962. In South Wales, the lofty Crumlin Viaduct carrying the Newport, Abergavenny and Hereford Railway across Ebbw Vale was demolished in 1965, removing from the South Wales scene a graceful iron structure that in places towered 200ft above the valley floor. Built between 1853 and 1857 to take a double-track line, it was reduced to single track in 1927 and finally closed in 1964.

The Belah, Deepdale and Crumlin Viaducts are now nothing but memories, but in Devon Meldon Viaduct remains intact at the time of writing, even though the track on the closed ex-LSWR Exeter-Plymouth main line has been removed. This Viaduct, constructed in 1874 just beyond Okehampton on the fringe of Dartmoor, is a graceful lattice structure and, like many of the bridges and viaducts already mentioned, seems to add to rather than detract from the surrounding scenery.

industries?

Despite the fact that the railways are the biggest single source of scrap, they are hardly the only source. If all redundant locomotives had been sold to one firm a dramatic, if localised, effect would have been observed. But they were not. In fact, even in the 1960s, locomotives were a mere fraction of BRs annual scrap output from redundant rolling stock and rails.

Mention has already been made of the redundancies caused by Modernisation. The BTC Report of 1954 forecast that Modernisation would have a "tonic effect upon staff morale of working with thoroughly modern and efficient apparatus". No doubt this prophecy has to some extent been fulfilled, but despite the improved conditions of railway work, much of the old 'camaraderie' of railway life has been lost in the process. Can we measure the improvements in railway marketing and the results which have been derived from the replacement of steam motive power? Would the present day "Inter-City" image be so attractive if the cleaning up that was possible once steam engines had gone had not been carried out? "Inter-City" gave BR a new image, and in 1968 they formally disassociated themselves from the old one. A major reason for the temporary "steam ban" at that time was to sever the connection in the minds of the public between old fashioned steam engines and modern railways. When the steam locomotive was eventually permitted to reappear to pull special excursions, few members of the public were in any doubt that they were anything other than museum pieces. The end of steam has had more effects on the railways of Britain than a general improvement in train times and speeds, yet how rarely do we see its indirect effects examined!

Dr. D. P. Williams recently wrote in *Railway World* that "It is highly probable that if B.R. had pursued a less vigorous programme of steam extinction . . . many fewer examples would be in active service on Britain's private lines today". I would beg to modify his views. The BTC Report reminded us that "the steam locomotive has in the past served the railway well", but "the technical re-equipment of the railways is long overdue" The steam engine, a device which had relatively little practical effect in the formative years of the Industrial Revolution in Britain, but which has come to symbolize that era of economic and social change, played a large if decreasing role in the 1960s. How many other major industries in Britain in the last two decades have placed such direct reliance on a seemingly outmoded form of power as did the railway industry? In contrast, the railways of the USA began large-scale dieselisation in the 1940s. If we are to be grateful for the fact that we have so many surviving examples of the steam locomotive we must be grateful not so much for the vigour with which BR replaced its steam fleet once it got the chance, but to the fact that in the immediate post-War years the railways were starved of finance and therefore had no opportunity to successfully compete with more flexible forms of transport. Had the railways been financially supported they may well have modernised their locomotive fleet at a time when British railway enthusiasts would have been unable to raise the capital to save a quarter of the number of engines now happily clattering about on preserved lines. The mass locomotive withdrawals of the 1960s may have benefitted the enthusiast, but they were certainly a long overdue requirement of the **railway industry.**

Tunnels — the inside story

W. T. Thornewell

Does anyone really, truthfully love a tunnel? Surely no 20th Century Board of Management or member of staff. Yet it is a remarkable fact that only a little more than a century ago, the Directors of more than one major company thought that a tunnel would be a public magnet, drawing in the crowds to their undertaking. Tunnels are definitely not nice, although I did know one man who loved the Severn Tunnel and was most disappointed when I refused the chance to see it at close quarters. I had seen the inside of far too many in my time to be enthusiastic about even this remarkable achievement!

But of course, tunnels are inevitable if a railway is to keep to modest gradients through hilly or mountainous country. The question of cost was, and is even more so now, a major factor in deciding whether a tunnel was constructed or merely a cutting, but at a higher level with steeper approach gradients. Again, the nature of the terrain is a potent factor; the London & Birmingham Railway decided on a long cutting at Tring, and an equally long tunnel at Kilsby. Whatever the considerations then, the tunnel was a difficult and costly proposition to maintain in the latter days of steam, whereas Tring cutting was an almost ideal stretch of track.

The new Woodhead Tunnel built at the time of the Manchester-Sheffield electrification in the 1950s alongside the original (and now disused) Great Central bores was a revelation for such as me, who had never seen a clean tunnel in a long association with them.

The Midland Railway had a lot of tunnels, and early in my official career I made intimate contact with one, Chevet by name. It was opened out almost 50 years ago, but in its heyday it was terrifying for the timid, very difficult to negotiate, and always full of smoke. Chevet was a bottleneck on the intensely busy but highly profitable stretch of track between Normanton and Cudworth. For two or three years before it was opened out, I was obliged to make weekly passages through it. In my estimation it was a 'three-hour' tunnel, for with a short stay with the gang working somewhere along its length, it took me three hours to cover its 702 yards.

It was always full of smoke, with seemingly hardly a moment when a train was not passing through it — expresses and local passenger trains, parcels and general freights, coal trains and empty wagon trains, even a few light engines — an endless flow of traffic. Relaying was a regular chore as, under this sort of traffic, the rails wore out quite often! When the LMS was formed and the Chief Engineer's Office was established at Euston, the LNW men soon decided that the answer to our problem was the use of Crewe rails from their own foundry — 60ft long, 85lb per yard and lovely to see. But nevertheless, under traffic they did not last as long as the Midland 45ft medium manganese rails. Chevet was a killer, a nuisance to all departments, and finally it was decided to open it out. It stole a march on us even then, for when work on the opening began, the rock through which it had been bored proved to be much harder than the trial borings had shown it to be — and that was bad enough, as we drilled away from a basket suspended down one of the smoke shafts! The completed widening provided the deepest cutting on the Midland lines.

At that time I little knew that for the best part of my career I should constantly be concerned with tunnels and the daily problems of

With a screech of its whistle and a roar of an exhaust fit to foul any tunnel, Fairburn Class 4 2-6-4T No 42282 heads into the smokey portal of Bangor Tunnel with a train for Pwllheli in June 1964. *K. Kneale*

their upkeep. In fact, the only time I had no tunnels to worry about was when I was at Carlisle in the war years. Everywhere else I was stationed I had tunnels to think about, and they were all, with one exception, rather horrible places, experienced from the inside. The exception was East Norton on the now closed GN and LNW Joint line between Welham Junction and Melton Mowbray.

East Norton was a lovely tunnel, wide and lofty and built on magnificent lines. Traffic through it consisted of a few passenger trains, the coal trains from Colwick to Willesden and the return empties. As there was usually a gentle breeze wafting through it, the smoke normally cleared immediately behind each train, and manholes were deep and plentiful. It could be said that it was in the general character of the other structures on the line, which were all built to very high standards — very much better, in fact, than those of either of the parent companies! In my own experience it was unique. It was possible when examining the track through it to completely relax from the cares of the outer world; all tunnels seem completely detached from the outside world, but it is only rarely that the detachment is a pleasant experience.

At Kelmarsh, Northants, the Southern end of the up line tunnel made a slight deflection to the left over the last 5 or 6 yards. I never discovered the reason for this, since the track both inside and outside the tunnel should have formed a continuous straight line. The kink in the alignment was clearly visible from an Officer's inspection car and usually required explanation. Not far away, Oxendon Down tunnel was found to require a complete roof repair, and as the alignment was curious to say the least, it was decided to both repair the roof and some side walls and then realign the track, which was curved. The job as finished was very good, but soon reports began to come in from drivers who variously alleged that the roof was coming in or that the track was foul of gauge. All reports proved to be unfounded, but it is most interesting that the previous much inferior conditions had never caused any misgivings among footplate staff. Needless to say, such philosophy does not come readily on a long and stormy walk in

113

the middle of the night to the site of the alleged complaint!

Life in tunnels is not all trouble, however — it has its lighter side. At a later period I had an Assistant who hated tunnels; his duties did not require him to specifically examine track or tunnels, so he normally avoided any contact with them. One day he had to get to a place on the other side of a 1200yd long tunnel, and he decided to walk over the top, through the fields. Halfway across the first field he suddenly saw an angry bull coming towards him — and he only just made it to the fence. Try as he would, he could not find a field where the bull did not also appear, and in the end the tunnel it had to be. Somehow, his cockney sense of humour could not cope with this rural episode, nor the subsequent cries of "toreador" which greeted him for some time afterwards!

Left: Hurrying out of the castellated north portal of Linslade Tunnel comes Class 86 No E3108 on the 12·15 Euston-Manchester via Birmingham on February 16, 1972. *J. H. Cooper-Smith*

Below: Into the blackness of Kilsby Tunnel goes rebuilt Royal Scot Class 4-6-0 No 6160 *Queen Victoria's Rifleman* with a Euston-Manchester express in LMS days. *H. Weston*

Conditions in tunnels vary widely. Some are appallingly wet, and others exceedingly dry. One day, one such dry tunnel suddenly sprung a jet of water of considerable and continuing force. We assumed that all the passenger trains which had passed through the tunnel after the jet started, soon after the afternoon routine inspection, must have had all their windows closed, for no complaints had been received from passengers or train crews! By improvisation, we managed to deflect the jet of water to track level. Inspection above the tunnel revealed that a local farmer had constructed a dam across a stream on the Railway Company's land, and the pent up waters were finding their way down through the lower rocks to emerge as a jet from the tunnel wall. Destruction of this unauthorised dam allowed the water to resume its normal course, and harmony was soon restored below.

Early in the Second World War, I was emerging from the end of a tunnel in Northamptonshire on my normal routine inspection when the soldier on guard, seeing my brightly polished tubular track gauge, took it for some secret and deadly weapon and kept me covered until his sergeant arrived, and I was able to proceed on my legitimate duty!

On the LNW main line there was one tunnel, a single bore, which at first sight seemed to be far too small to take a train, although reason indicated that it must be correctly built to the structure gauge. When the big Coronation Pacifics entered this tunnel they drove the air in front of them with such force that the air-eruption at the outgoing end would carry any unsecured object a few hundred yards down the line, seriously alarming anyone near the track and new to this extraordinary happening. It was safe to be in the tunnel, as long as you were at least halfway through it and standing well back in a manhole. Nobody was permitted to enter the tunnel except at specified times and with a competent guide from the track gang. Well ensconced in a manhole at a safe location, it was a terrific experience when a Pacific hit the entrance at 80mph. On the footplate, you covered your nose, mouth and ears for the few seconds of the enormous air displacement. There were other hazards to the men on the track, but these were well understood and safely coped with. Nevertheless this tunnel ranked as a place requiring the utmost care and knowledge when working inside to avoid an early demise.

Elsewhere, an odd method of widening had produced a situation in which two single bore tunnels flanked a double bore in the centre. It can easily be seen that, with tracks arranged up down up down, trains passing through the centre tunnel ran on the right-hand track. This caused endless trouble with official visitors who in the blackness of the tunnel forgot the unusual arrangement, and had to be repeatedly prevented from walking with their backs to oncoming traffic.

One of the most alarming situations was a tunnel where a main road ran exactly parallel but at a higher level on the hillside. The faint rumble of road traffic was disconcerting and made it difficult to distinguish between a train entering the distant end of the tunnel and an unusually heavy and noisy lorry on the road above. It was a time for caution; it was no picnic to be in this tunnel with its intrusive road noises when a heavy coal train came in complete with a banker to add to the oppressive blackness with two lots of steam, smoke and noise.

Carefully selected times, when there are few trains about or the wind is in the right direction, offer the best opportunities for tunnel inspection, but this is not always possible. Often one had to go at a bad time for commencing the walk through the tunnel, perhaps on a day when the wind was blowing across the entrances, keeping the smoke more or less trapped inside the tunnel, apart from what escaped up the smoke shafts. It is on such a day that I have to conduct a novice through a tunnel that is well known for its blackness and volume of traffic, and which is more than

a mile long, wet throughout and curved all the way!

Walking into this tunnel (and many others), everything changes. All natural light disappears within a few yards and one is swallowed up in complete blackness, surrounded by thick eddying smoke. Almost at once my companion stumbles over a pile of ballast and, his hand going out to the wall to steady himself, quickly commences the aquisition of the inevitable tunnel patina of soot and grease.

The area around our feet illuminated by the handlamps is very small, and the sooty blackness seems to swallow all light above rail level. We listen and then resume our walk, but before we have gone 40 yards a muffled noise in the distance proclaims the entrance of a train at the far end of the tunnel, and immediately, with careful unfaltering steps, we make for a manhole I had noted a second before. Hardly have we gained our sooty

Top: The combination of length, single-track bores and a predominantly damp climate made an evil reputation for the Great Central's original Woodhead Tunnels, now superseded by the double-track bore built for the Manchester-Sheffield electrification in 1954. Some idea of the foul conditions inside the tunnel can be gauged from the smoke and steam billowing out of the opposite tunnel mouth as two 4-4-0s hurry west in this view of the eastern portal in Great Central days. *LPC Collection*

Centre: Not only do engineers have to regularly check every inch of main running tunnels, but also all drainage and ventilation shafts. Here, during an occupation of Caerphilly Tunnel, Western Region staff prepare to inspect one of the ventilation shafts in a specially-designed cradle. *British Rail*

Bottom: That was a tunnel that was! When Broomhouse tunnel north of Chesterfield on the Midland main line to Sheffield needed attention in 1969, it was decided to open it out instead. So the soil was removed from above, the line was temporarily closed to traffic in mid-August so that the track through the tunnel could be lifted, then the entire structure was demolished with explosives. A month later trains were running again and only the very discerning passenger could now detect that there had ever been a tunnel there. *British Rail*

refuge than an express hurries past on the opposite track, its smoke and steam quite veiling from us even a glimpse of the passengers enjoying their coffee or perhaps reading a book. All we see are dimly flashing lights as it hurries past — and suddenly it is gone and eerie silence descends again. But not completely, for slightly louder than before we begin to hear the approach of the train on the track nearest to us, evidently from the sound a heavily loaded mineral train with its usual powerful engine at the head. As we wait quietly in the pitch darkness, the engine clatters past us, adding its contribution to the unpleasant mixture we are already breathing. The wagons rumble by and in a few moments we are yet again in the uncanny silent black world of swirling smoke and steam. On such a day the smoke will eddy back and forth all the time, playing games around our lamps if we lift them to eye-level in a fruitless attempt to see more about us. There is no point in waiting for a clearance, for this is a busy line, so we listen intently and then quietly and carefully press on towards the centre of the tunnel, stopping every 10 yards or so to listen, always with a manhole at hand. A faint sound begins to grow in magnitude and I urge my companion into the nearby recess. Yes, a train is coming, and as we wait I tell my novice colleague of the colour light intermediate block home signal towards the north end of the tunnel which allows trains to come through at rather more frequent intervals then might be thought. By now he has accepted the desirability of limited and subdued conversation whilst we are walking, so that we can keep our minds and senses constantly alert for our own safety. Silence is golden in that intense blackness — in every sense!

After almost six hours of walking and waiting, we emerge from the other end, tired and dirty, but having in the meanwhile examined the rails under the smoke shafts and measured them (and having accumulated a lot of dirt and grime in the process!), inspected the catchpits of the "six foot" drain, noted that some man-holes were not well indicated and needed repainting, and generally checked that the rails throughout were well above the minimum weight allowed. In our travels we have also noted some fishplates and elastic rail spikes that needed to be renewed, but had thankfully discovered only two broken baseplates.

Outside was another world, where men lived, the sun shone and time ticked along normally; where we had been for the past six hours there was an absence of all normal dimensions. Putting out our lamps, we place them in the nearby lamp room and lock it up, before indulging in a welcome wash to rid ourselves of the worst of the grime. Next a drink of the ice cold, sparkling water which springs from the sides of the rocky cutting, for suddenly we realise we have had nothing to eat or drink all day!

Nowadays, of course, the atmosphere in tunnels tends to be a little cleaner, especially if there is a predominance of electric trains. But except in the newest or relined tunnels, much of the soot and grime of the steam era remains, occasionally to come showering down when dislodged by a fiercer than usual diesel exhaust. As far as safety is concerned one has to be even more alert nowadays, for with a combination of welded rails, higher running speeds and quieter locomotives, trains can be upon you before you know it. In this sense, a good, bright lamp is a valuable asset, for locomotive crews seeing a light moving in a tunnel will always give a blast on the horn to warn of their approach.

I am never sure which was the dirtiest job I had to do — the regular fortnightly examination of the tunnels I had to maintain, or the occasional 100mph dash on an express engine, in theory to test the condition and stability of the track, but all too often in fact rocking and swaying along to such an extent that it was all too obvious that the engine was nearing shopping time, and making a nonsense of my journey! But I know which was the most thrilling!

Shy '65

E. J. Alyson

"Are you ready then, Jacko?" called Tom across the office. "And we'll have no mucking about on this trip lad," he continued "I want to be home in double quick time tonight for that darts match." Tom was only joking. He was a careful, conscientious driver, and although he didn't hang about, he was not the sort to take risks, even for his beloved darts team. As we picked up our gear and set off down the platform, one of the other drivers suggested with a straight face that perhaps we ought to delay Tom so as to give his team a better chance of winning!

I had been Tom's regular fireman for the past 18 months, and although there was the best part of 40 years between us, he was a kind and gentle man and we got on famously. Earlier in the afternoon we had worked up with a Standard 4 on a leisurely parcels turn, and Tom was quite happy to let me take the regulator while he looked after the fire. Now we were booked to take the 5.43 pm commuter train back — a heavyish job of 11 bogies, but no problem for the usual Pacific or Class 5. It had been drizzling in the afternoon, and now with the onset of darkness, it had turned to a steady downpour. As we stood at the platform end, collars turned up against the weather, waiting for the shed crew to bring in our loco, Tom was musing about his tactics for the match, while I was beginning to worry about how much time I wasn't going to have to get the fire to my liking before we were due out. Eventually, however, a flickering oil lamp picked its way out from amidst the bright lights of the continuously toing and froing suburban electric trains and behind it materialised the shape of a rather grimy Pacific, backing cautiously down onto our train. As she came to a stand, it was immediately obvious that all was not well; instead of two cheerful faces to greet us on the footplate, there were worried frowns and apologies. And Tom, spotting the number beneath the grime, winked and said, "Now's your chance Jacko — they've lumbered us with '65." I'd not fired on '65 before, for she was not really one of our engines. But I'd heard that, along with two other members of her otherwise free-steaming Class, '65 had a reputation for steaming only when she felt like it. And tonight, quite evidently, was one of her off days. Instead of a nice bright fire, water in the top half of the glass, and pressure just high enough to lift a wisp of steam from the safety valves, I was about to inherit from an apologetic colleague one very black fire, a gauge glass looking as forlorn as an empty gin bottle, pressure struggling around the 150 mark — and little more than ten minutes before the off. And just to add a little sport to the proceedings, I was told the right hand injector didn't seem to be working at all! While Tom got to work with the blower, I tried to prod some flames of enthusiasm from the fire and, intermittently, wrestled with the reluctant injector.

Ten minutes later, when the colour light on the gantry above the chimney flicked to green, we had gained a few pounds in the boiler and pushed the water level up a bit, but I was far from happy with the fire. "Right," said Tom, "Let's see what she'll do." A series of whistles from down the platform, last minute commuters hastily slamming doors behind them, a green lamp held aloft, and we were away. And straight away '65 picked up her wheels in a violent bout of slipping. No sanding was allowed leaving the terminus, but luckily the little tank that had brought our empty stock in was giving us a shove at the back, and Tom managed to check the slipping before we quite came to a stand. "That" said Tom "should pull your fire round." But it didn't. Still hardly a flicker from that great black heap inside the firedoors!

In between violent bouts of slipping (in the course of which we made another discovery — the sanders were not working either) we slowly got under way, winding our train of commuters and early Christmas shoppers through the metropolis back to their outer suburban homes. Tom deliberately took it easily through the inner suburbs, hoping to give me an opportunity to get the fire going. But I began to feel, as an electric train contemptuously overtook us on the slow line, that things did not look too bright. Ahead, as far as the eye could see, green colour lights twinkled through the rain, their strong beams sending reflections dancing along the rails towards us. The preceding fast electric had certainly shown us a clean pair of heels, and since it was usual practice to run through this area on a string of double-yellows, I could imagine the tail-back that was building up behind us as we crawled slowly from section to section. I eventually had to admit that for reasons I could not understand, I was making no progress at all — what little steam I was able to raise I was having to use to keep a reasonable amount of water in the glass.

"Okay" said Tom "if she won't pull round with kindness, we'll have to try a spot of cruelty!" And with that, he opened the regulator wide; '65 responded at first, surging forward with a renewed strength. But it was a final fling — despite the raucous blast from the chimney, pressure began to drop spectacularly, the fire remained imperturbably dull and the water in the glass gave every indication that it was about to do a vanishing trick. Glumly, Tom announced that we would have to stop for a blow-up. A blow-up! On the main line in the rush hour! This was going to take some living down.

We were in the outer suburbs now, just beyond the limit of the colour-light area and back in semaphore country. With a warning blast on the whistle, Tom brought the train to a stand opposite the next box, and while he climbed down and ducked through the rain to tell the startled signalman what was afoot, I set to work yet again on the fire. I tried every trick I knew — and in desperation one or two others besides. Slowly, very slowly, she began to pull round. Meanwhile, a long procession of delayed electric trains began to rumble past on the adjacent slow line, diverted around us by the signalman at the previous box. Each was preceded by a disapproving blast on their electric horns, and from every one bored faces peered at us through rain-speckled windows. Tom returned from the box just as the 6 o'clock down, itself headed by a Pacific, came gently up alongside. Just to make my day, who should be peering out from the cab but my arch rugby opponent Sylvan Jones. "Having trouble, then, Jacko boy" he said innocently in his sing-song accent as they rumbled by. Luckily for his tender ears, he did not hear my somewhat basic riposte!

In another five minutes, Tom was ready to try again. "If we can clear the main line" he said "we shall be alright." He was right for, once off the main line, apart from the short climb up through the tunnel, it was gently downhill practically all the way home. With a blast on the whistle to let the signalman know we were ready, we got underway again, although not without some bad bouts of slipping (still no sand!) and a display of pyrotechnics which, had it not been for the teaming · rain, would no doubt have been spectacular. By dint of very gentle running, and taking maximum advantage of the favourable gradients, we managed to clear the main line without a further stop, albeit now running almost three-quarters of an hour late.

We now began the short, sharp climb up through the tunnel which, in normal circumstances we would rush through without any trouble, but which on this day was going

120

to be rather more formidable. Several times on the climb '65 picked up her wheels, but Tom was ready at the regulator and corrected the slip each time before it had a chance to develop. Instead of bowling through the tunnel at the usual 50 mph, we eventually struggled into the yawning portals at something below 20 mph. Almost immediately, the cab was filled with thick, swirling smoke and noxous fumes from our nonetoo healthy fire, and both Tom and I were obliged to crouch on the cab floor in order to breathe anything resembling fresh air. Once more '65 lost her feet, and although Tom made a quick grab for the regulator, the resultant outpouring from the chimney did nothing to improve our environment. Luckily, the tunnel is not long, and eventually we emerged once again into the black, rainsoden winter landscape. I leaned out of the cab to take a few gulps of fresh air and to get a glimpse of the distant for the next level crossing for Tom, because it was sited in a cutting on a long, gentle right-handed curve and therefore impossible to see from the driver's side on a big-boilered engine. Not, I mused, as I peered through the stinging rain for the flickering light, that we had any need to worry about our braking even if it was "on," for although we were now beginning to run downhill we were still barely doing more than 30 mph. Suddenly, through the rain, I caught a fleeting glimpse of a flickering white light low down on the track. This was a very rural stretch of line, and there were no houses or street lights for miles around, so I had just decided that it must be the Tilley lamp of some unfortunate trackman called out on this filthy night when, next instant, I caught sight of a very indistinct red light just beyond! "Look out Tom, it looks like there's a red light up ahead" I called. In a second Tom was across the cab and peering out beside me. In another he was back again, slamming the regulator shut, dropping the brake handle and swinging on the sanding valve lever in one movement, while at the same time yelling to

me to keep my head down.

Good old '65 had spent the entire evening resisting our attempts to get her to move, and now she was being asked to stop she responded happily — the sanding gear we had spent all our time trying to persuade to work now functioned without a murmur. As we came rapidly but smoothly to a stand, without a trace of a slide, we saw to our horror that immediately ahead our path was blocked by a petrol tanker lying on its side amidst the mangled remains of the parapit of the bridge from which it had crashed. The flickering white light I had seen was in fact the tankers' damaged battery shorting against the metal frame, while the dim red lights were its flickering tail lamps. And even as we climbed down from '65, by now at a stand only feet short of the obstruction, the battery exploded and the tanker burst into flame. Tom dashed forward to drag the unconscious driver from his wrecked cab and yelled to me to reverse the train clear. I climbed back aboard, wrenched '65 into reverse and yanked the regulator open. She instantly obeyed, and to cap it all, the safety valves lifted defiantly.

In due course the emergency services arrived, summoned by a passing motorist, and we could return to our by now thoroughly-disgruntled passengers to await the arrival of an Ivatt 'Mickey Mouse' tank to pilot us back "wrong line" through the tunnel to the junction where we took water before setting out once more — now over three hours late.

Tom, needless to say, missed his darts match, but we had no more trouble with '65 that night — she behaved perfectly, steaming happily all the rest of the way home. It was almost as if she had known there was trouble ahead, and was determined not to get involved. Certainly, on the many occasions that I fired and drove '65 subsequently, there was no recurrence of the trouble we had that night. And whenever I heard crews complaining about her bad steaming, I used to chuckle and wonder what trouble '65 had been keeping herself out of this time!

Salisbury to Exeter

Centre left: The low winter sun catches the sidesheets of BR Standard Class 5 4-6-0 No 73114 as it canters into Sherborne with an up stopping train on November 8 1958. *B. A. Poley*

Bottom left: On Summer Saturdays it was often necessary to run the 'Atlantic Coast Express' in two, three or even four portions, even at the time when the Western Region took over. This is the Plymouth portion, loaded to the maximum of 13 coaches that Waterloo could accommodate, heading west near Wilton behind rebuilt Battle of Britain Pacific No 34082 *615 Squadron* on a busy Saturday in August 1961. *G. Smith*

Below: Heading west: without a trace of a slip, Rebuilt Merchant Navy Class 4-6-2 No 35001 *Channel Packet* pulls smartly away from Salisbury with the down Atlantic Coast Express on April 2 1962. *R. N. Joanes*

Top left: The Salisbury-Exeter line was the Southern Region's West of England main line, and formed almost the only connection between its empire in Devon and North Cornwall west of Exeter and the remainder of the system east of Salisbury. It was a steeply graded but well engineered line, and served many places en route, with several branches to East Devon coastal resorts. In the Beeching Era, however, when the alternative routes to the West were being considered for rationalisation, the Western Region saw the existence of the Salisbury-Exeter main line as a threat to their own route via Newbury and Westbury, which generally traversed far less populous country. It was not surprising, therefore, that when the Western Region gained control of all the Southern lines west of Salisbury, it set about disabling its competitor with singular verve; first the branch lines to Lyme Regis, Seaton, Sidmouth and Exmouth via Budleigh Salterton were closed and lifted over a few short years, then several of the main line stations themselves were closed and demolished, and finally the main line itself was singled throughout apart from the short section between the site of Templecombe station and Yeovil Junction. Although the line is still maintained to main line standards, the single line sections preclude fast through running, whilst their length dictates a basically two-hourly service; almost all through freight from Salisbury to the West has to travel the longer ex-GWR route via Westbury, including reversal there. Such are the internal politics of a supposedly unified National railway system! One of the first manifestations of the Western Region influence was the splitting up of the Southern's standard coaching stock formations. Here, just a year after the change of management, unrebuilt West Country Class Pacific No 34099 *Lynmouth* finds itself in charge of a Bulleid brake composite freshly repainted in lined maroon and an ex-LNER Thompson corridor second as it emerges from Honiton Tunnel and begins the descent to Seaton Junction with a stopping train from Exeter on September 5 1964. *Paul Riley*

Top: In later years, the Exmouth and Sidmouth branches were the domain of BR Standard Class 3 2-6-2Ts, although restrictions continued to preclude them from the Seaton and Lyme Regis lines. The Exmouth direct line was more suburban in character than the others, and enjoyed a considerable morning and evening commuter traffic, usually worked with non-corridor stock, as was this train leaving Exeter for Exmouth behind 2-6-2Ts No 82017 and 82019 on June 27 1959. *S. Creer*

Above: Swinging across into the down through platform at Exeter Central is U Class 2-6-0 No 31633 piloting S15 4-6-0 No 30845 with a train from Axminster on June 27 1959. *S. Creer*

Top right: In their rebuilt form, the Bulleid Pacifics were at first banned west of Exeter — from the very tracks for which they were originally designed! Later, they were allowed to work through to Plymouth — though never on the North Devon lines — and it is at the head of an up Plymouth express that No 34024 *Tamar Valley* approaches Exeter St Davids and passes W Class 2-6-4T No 31911 in the banker's siding. *R. C. Riley*

Centre right: Southern Region trains from Plymouth and North Devon had to traverse Western Region tracks between Cowley Bridge Junction and Exeter St Davids before attacking the sharply curved incline up to their own station at Exeter Central. For several years, Maunsell Z Class 0-8-0Ts served as bankers over this stretch; here No 30954 together with N Class 2-6-0 No 31832 pushes a heavy Waterloo-bound express out of St Davids on August 30, 1959. *G. England*

Bottom right: *Exeter* at Exeter: the first of Bulleid's light Pacifics, No 34001 *Exeter* rolls an up train from North Devon into St Davids on a wet day in the early 50s while in the siding alongside, an E1R 0-6-2T waits to bank the train up through the tunnel to Central Station.